Y0-CAV-840

Blood on Red Dirt

The true story of a Marine Corporal in Vietnam 1968

By

Gary K. Cowart

Copyright © 2012 Gary K. Cowart

All rights reserved.

ISBN: 1468147579
ISBN-13: 978-1468147575

Prelude to War

For those who have to fight

for it, life has a flavor the

Protected will never know.

(Engraved Vietnam Zippo lighter)

Dedicated to the men, living and dead, of

3rd Battalion, 11th Marines, 1st Marine Div.

USMC

***

By the same author

PROLOGUE, 21 AUGUST 1968

Quang Nam Province Vietnam, 0753

It was hot for so early in the morning. I was hot and uncomfortable, holding a 105mm howitzer round on my shoulder as I knelt in the tall grass next to the LZ at Thoung Duc Special Forces Camp. It was heavy and I was tired. It was my third visit to this hellhole, and I was scared. I was glad I was going to be on the first CH-46 Sea Knight chopper out of here. I couldn't get out fast enough. I hated this place.

I sat there looking at a group of 7th Marines across the landing zone and thinking back at all the events in my life that put me in this little patch of grass in this obscure little country at this particular time.

I could see and hear the Sea Knights now, a few miles away, and I thought of my situation, and the circumstances of my life that I could control and could not control. I thought of how so many events had to merge into one path to get an individual to a certain place and a certain time. How it all had to work out or fate would take you another direction. This was my path and I could do little to adjust my course.

I would never wish the Vietnam War on anyone, or any conflict for that matter, but I would never trade my experience here for anything. Six months and twenty-one days. Two hundred and one days in the country, and I still had a hundred and eighty days to go.

No, I would never forget Vietnam. It was now a part of me just like my brain, my mind, and my soul, never to be taken away until life itself ends. And life can end in a heartbeat, especially in this place.

Remember to always count your blessings when things are good, and to count them twice when things are bad.

This is my story.

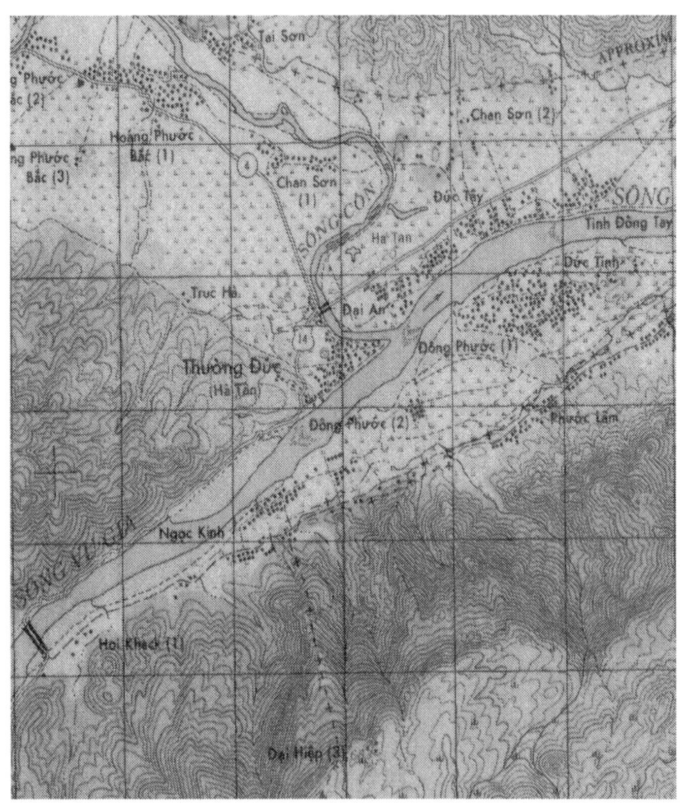

Tai Sơn
Chan Sơn (2)
Hoàng Phước
Bắc (1)
Bắc (3)
Chan Sơn
(1)
Đức Tây
SÔNG CÔN
Hà Tân
Tinh Đông Tây
Đức Tinh
Trúc Hà
Đại An
14
Thường Đức
(Hà Tân)
Đông Phước (1)
Đông Phước (2)
Phước Lâm
Ngọc Kinh
Hội Khách (1)
Đại Hiệp (3)

Thuong Duc

A TIME TO FEAR

1965 was a great time to be a teenager. It was a time of carefree existence. It was also the peak of America's love for the big fast automobile, and boys like me were finding a way to afford our own car. It was a time of cruising the main street of town to the sounds of the Beach Boys, looking for cute girls, and weekends full of hamburgers and French fries and chocolate malts. And the times were truly changing, as Bob Dylan sang. It was a time of civil rights, free love, and Beatle haircuts. Everything was in tune for the exciting change from adolescent to adulthood for millions of Baby Boomers, with one exception: a small country no one had ever heard of was having a civil war, and America, for questionable reasons, was escalating its presence in this civil war of ideology.

The Vietnam War was about to tear the United States apart, and millions of young men and women found themselves scrambling to find out what to do about it. I was no exception. I was afraid of dying in war. I had plans for my future and a new girlfriend I adored. As I sat in my high school classes in the fall of 1964, my plan was to go to college and get a deferment from military duty. I wanted to become a Forest Ranger and marry my sweetheart. Many of my friends at those times were joining the military reserve at the insistence of their fathers. At the time I thought this was stupid; I wanted no part of the military or war. Frankly, I was afraid, but I was also feeling a bit guilty because both my mom and my dad had served in WWII, and my grandfather had served in WWI. However, my brains would keep me out of this war. Or so I thought.

As my eighteenth birthday passed, I signed up for the required Selective Service Department (The Draft) and graduated from high school in the spring of 1965. I wasted no time in signing up for classes at Green River Community College in Washington State, and I continued my part-time job working for Ivar's Restaurant on Broadway Avenue in Seattle. I also took another job at the local Shell Oil gas station pumping gas during the morning commute. Between the two jobs, I hoped to make enough money to pay for tuition for the coming year. My mother and stepfather made it clear that I could continue to live at home while in college, but they would pay for no college expenses. Higher education was not a priority for them.

Things didn't go as planned, and after a summer of hard work I only had about forty percent of what was needed for a whole year of college. When classes started, I quit my restaurant job but kept the morning gas-pumping job for spending money. I quickly found that college work was not as easy as I thought. The Selective Service required a full load of classes, and with a part-time job and all the normal distractions of friends and college life, my grades were not what I had hoped. I barely got Cs in all my classes, and at the end of the first quarter I was broke and disappointed with myself. I had no money for the next quarter of school so I took a leave of absence and went to work full time at a cement plant making conduit pipe.

This was a great job. It paid $1.96 an hour, which was a lot then, and I was able to save enough money for two more quarters of school. One downfall was the fact that since I was no longer in school, my stepfather made me pay $50 a month toward room and board. Still, I was able to enroll in spring quarter and to get my deferment reinstated. My grades still were not up to my expectations, but I was maintaining above a C average thanks to an A in a bowling class, and a C average or above was all I needed for graduation.

Things were looking good until my girlfriend of fifteen months broke up with me for another boy. I was crushed. I was depressed. That summer session I took only one class and worked to save more money for school. By the time fall quarter started I was in very good shape financially and had a 2.2 grade point average. Once again, I kept the gas station job for spending money and set out to finish my first year of credits. Things were going better, and I had met new friends. I was taking varsity cross-country along with my other classes and doing quite well. My grades were at B level, and my life seemed to be humming. We finished the cross-country season two weeks before final exams, and I received my varsity letterman's jacket for free. I loved that jacket. Still have it in my closet today.

The weekend before finals, in late November 1966, a bunch of us were going to take a break from studies and go to a dance on Saturday night. It was a fun distraction, and we all had a good time. My parents were out of town for the weekend with their travel trailer so I didn't have to worry about coming in late and waking them up. It turned into a stormy night, and as I was driving a friend home, the weather got worse.

After I dropped my friend off, a few miles from my house, I was going down a hill in a pouring rainstorm. Visibility was poor. A car pulled out ahead of me towing another car. It was raining very hard, with standing water on the road. I assumed the other cars would gain speed so I didn't slow down much. All of a sudden I realized that they were not moving. When I panicked and slammed on the brakes, my bald tires slid over the wet road, and I smashed my 1957 Ford into the rear end of the towed vehicle. My head hit the steering wheel, breaking out an upper left canine tooth and causing lots of bleeding.

As a result, I ended up in the local hospital for a few days with a concussion. My smashed car was towed to the Redondo Heights garage and parked in the front parking area where my parents couldn't miss seeing it the next day when they came back from their trip. Aside from the concussion and the broken tooth, I healed quickly and was out of the hospital by Wednesday. However, I missed my finals.

Since my car was totaled, I got a ride the next day from a friend and took the accident report and my hospital charges to the college as proof that I had an excuse to miss my finals. To no avail.

They wouldn't even talk to me! No excuses were accepted for missing finals. I went to the Dean and requested permission to take my finals late. No exceptions. Two weeks later I received my grades: four F's and an A in cross-country. My grade point average dropped below a 1.8 out of 4.0 possible, and if that wasn't bad enough, they included a letter telling me I was dismissed academically and would have to wait another full quarter before I could apply for reinstatement.

A dreary Christmas passed, and I got a letter from the Selective Service telling me I had lost my college deferment and was now classified 1-A for the draft. I had no other alternative than to get a job and wait to see if I could avoid the draft until I could get back into college. A week after my twentieth birthday in early February 1967, I received my draft notice.

I was crushed. I had an uneasy feeling that I might not survive Vietnam, and I certainly didn't want to die in that war. I thought of my real father and felt so alone. It would have been a good time to talk to a dad about fear. I thought about talking to my mother or my step dad, but they had never had any desire to talk with me before, so I just lay awake that whole first night thinking. I thought of my grandfather in WWI, and my parents, uncles, and aunts in WWII, and at some point early in the morning, I came to the realization that I must confront my fear and move on.

The next day I talked to my best friend Gregg, and he said that he had been planning to talk to the different services to see if he could get a better job by enlisting prior to being drafted. So Gregg and I went to the Coast Guard, Navy, and Air Force, and they all had one to two year waiting lists for the regular four-year enlistment. The Army was better, but not much. I didn't want the Marine Corps because the Marines were in the thick of battle before anyone else, and, as I said, I was afraid.

Finally, Gregg and I went to the Marine Corps anyway. It was our last choice, but there was no waiting list. The recruiter was a tough looking guy, a few years older than us, but not very big. He knew we were hesitant and afraid. He sat us down and gave it to us straight. If we joined the Corps we would go to Vietnam and probably go into combat. He said the advantages were that we only had to serve two years. Six months of training, thirteen months in Vietnam, and then we would be eligible for four years paid college. He said we would receive the best training and that we would gain self-confidence and courage.

"You're not little boys any more. Momma won't be with you. You will thank yourselves some day if you join," he said. He was right.

I was ashamed of my fear and made the commitment right there. Gregg made it as well, and the next day another friend, Mike, joined us and the three of us went in on the buddy system to boot camp. We would not have to leave until August 7th, 1967, which gave us almost six months to work and have fun. The recruiter took my draft paperwork and said he would take care of it. I left the recruiting office still afraid, but with a new pride in myself. I could deal with the fear now.

I had told my mom and step dad about my draft notice and about joining the Marine Corp, and they thought I should have joined the Air Force or Navy instead. I was proud that I hadn't because I saw the fear in their eyes. Besides I couldn't get by the two-year waiting list. I wanted this challenge now; I wanted to continue to challenge my fear.

The next six months were filled with some of the best times in my life up to that point. I got a new job at a Richfield gas station in Burien, Washington for two dollars an hour and bought an old 1952 Ford station wagon to replace my wrecked car. Gregg and Mike were already working, and we had plenty of time on the weekends for going to dances and meeting new girls.

The months went by quickly, filled with drag racing at Puyallup raceways, rock concerts, dances, and girls. I saved no money. There was a new girl that I had met at the gas station. She was a senior in high school, and she walked past the station everyday after school. I noticed her, but was always too busy to say anything. One day the boss was gone and I was working alone. She stopped in to buy a Coke, and we talked. The next two days she came by for small talk, and I finally asked if she wanted to go out for a burger and fries on Friday after work.

She was a nice girl and seemed to like me a lot, but my heart was still with my old girlfriend even though she was still with the other guy. I didn't see the old girlfriend that summer, but did call her parents and went to visit them before I went to boot camp. They treated me different. They seemed actually glad to see me, and in so many words told me they were sorry how things worked out, but their daughter was young, as was I, and they said if things were meant to be, we could still have a friendship later. I felt good that they had given me encouragement and a cause to make it home after Vietnam.

The day of departure came all too soon. Gregg, Mike and I stayed at my house the last night, all three of us sleeping on my bed. We left early that morning for downtown Seattle and the Federal Building where we were directed to a large room full of other young men. They lined us up in rows and gave us our military pledge to the United States and our Commander In Chief.

We were split up into service groups. The first group was a small group of three or four for the Coast Guard. The next were good-sized groups for the Navy and Air Force, and then they called for the Army. This was the largest group of all, and when they left, there were three of us still in the room. Mike, Gregg, and me. We were the only Marines out of all those guys. The Federal man came over and took out a yellow manila envelope with our orders and called out our names. He called mine last and said that since I was the oldest, by three months, I would carry the envelope to San Diego. He told us we would be taking a van to the airport, and we could call our families with the flight information, so they could meet us and say their goodbyes.

It was a sunny afternoon, and I had my mom, younger brother, and grandmother there to say goodbye. My current girlfriend came later with some other friends, and it seemed like a party. Mike, Gregg and I had never been on a 707 jet before so we were excited about that as well. Soon it was time to board, and we hugged and kissed our family and friends. They all cried.

We found that we had seats in the first row behind first class, and the flight attendants knew who and what we were so they gave us a little extra attention. The plane took off just as the sun was setting, and by the time we reached San Diego it was very dark. As the plane was parking, the head flight attendant told us which way to go to find the Marine Corps counter inside the terminal.

We were all tired because we had not slept well the night before, and as we got off the plane our excitement grew. I had the yellow envelope and took the lead. Soon we saw two Marines in khaki dress and Smokey Bear hats behind a tall counter and headed for them. They saw the envelope and our shaggy Beatle haircuts and smiled at one another. I came up to the counter and handed them the yellow envelope, and I said, "I guess I give this to you guys."

The older of the two took the envelope and smiled at me as I leaned against the counter to ease my tired body. The Marine sergeant looked at me as he opened the envelope and asked in a pleasant voice if I was tired.

I thought to myself, “These guys aren’t so bad,” and looked back at Mike and Gregg before I replied that “yes, we were all pretty tired.”

The sergeant then leaned closer to me and his smiled changed slightly, just enough to let me know that all was not what it seemed.

“Well, I’m sorry you’re so tired with the long flight and all,” he whispered. “But . . . ,” (and then his voice rose) “get the F*** off my desk and stand at attention!”

I can only remember thinking, “Oh shit, now it begins.”

The other Marine started around the counter, spewing profanity, and getting us into line. When he gave us a command, he yelled at us, because we didn’t say, “AYE, AYE, SIR!”

We did a left face and began marching down the corridor toward the main street entrance of the terminal. The Drill Instructor yelled at us the whole time as we marched past countless civilians who seemed to pay us little or no attention, like it was the most common occurrence of their day.

And it was for those who lived in San Diego in 1967. They were accustomed to seeing Marine recruits.

The D.I. marched us outside where we noticed a few more recruits already standing at attention curbside. We joined them and after a good dressing down by the Drill Instructor, a warning not to move a muscle, and another "Aye, aye, sir," he left us. It was surreal. People came and went paying no attention to us, like we were invisible. Soon the D.I. returned with five more men, and so it went for what seemed liked hours until there were more than eighty young men standing at attention in front of the San Diego Airport terminal building. What on earth had I let myself in for?

MARINE CORPS BOOT CAMP

I was so tired. I could feel my body faltering in the wind, and I felt that if this didn't end soon I would pass out. I kept waiting for those near me to break ranks or talk or faint or something to just break the monotony. None did. Neither did I. It must have been all of eleven o'clock in the evening when the green buses pulled up. The main drill instructor came out in front of us. He looked at us long and hard before he spoke.

"When I give you maggots the word, I want to see you move double time into those buses. Do you understand?"

"Aye, aye, sir," we answered.

"I can't hear you ladies!" he bellowed.

"AYE, AYE, SIR!" We responded much louder than the first time. It was a scenario we would repeat countless times in the next seven weeks.

"When I give the word, I want to see nothing but assholes and elbows. Do you understand?"

This was another phrase that we would come to love and cherish in the coming weeks.

"Aye, aye, sir!"

"I can't hear you pukes!"

"AYE, AYE, SIR!" we responded.

"Ready....move!"

At the command, "Move!" eighty some-odd recruits ran as fast as we could to the nearest bus. We clambered into the bus, falling into seats until they were all taken. A few recruits had to run back off and find another bus with empty seats. Just as I was starting to relax, another D.I. hopped on the bus yelling and screaming.

"No one told you maggots to sit down," he roared, as he began pulling the nearest recruits to their feet. In short order we were all standing. Satisfied, he returned to the front of the bus.

"When I give the word, I want you all to sit at once with a smack!" He smacked his thigh with his hand for emphasis.

"Ready....sit!" he yelled.

We didn't exactly sit as one, and as he spewed more profanity, there were more aye, ayes. After more tries at sitting, we finally got it in our heads that he wanted us to smack our thighs loudly with our hands as we sat. After a dozen tries, or, more likely after the last bus was ready, we performed the sit to his satisfaction and the bus moved out. It was the last relaxation I would have for the next thirty hours. Too bad the bus ride only lasted fifteen minutes.

It was very late when we arrived at Marine Corps Recruit Depot and ran off the bus onto a pair of yellow footprints painted on the concrete. I thought that we would be going to bed soon, and that is all that kept me going. First, they had us run two and three at a time into a lighted room around the corner, and we came back out with no hair. My haircut lasted less than ten seconds.

When the haircuts were finished, they marched us single file into a large room full of tables with two-foot square, three-sided cubicles on them. The open side faced out. As ordered, we had picked up a cardboard box on the way in the door and had stood at attention in front of a cubicle, one to a customer. We stood and stood and stood. There were a few Marines walking around the room yelling on occasion at someone to get back to attention. These were not drill instructors, but regular Marines. At some point they passed out mailing labels, and we filled them out, a few of us at a time, while the others stood at attention. This went on for hours with a few guys fainting from the exhaustion. I kept moving my toes and swaying a little to keep my blood circulating. Finally after everyone had addressed the mailing labels, we were told to strip and put everything in the box except our wallets. Each wallet of each man was searched, and the only allowable items left in it were a driver's license, a social security card and, I think, dollars in paper cash. There may have been a limit on how much money was allowed; I can't remember.

Everything else in the wallet was either going home to momma or would be confiscated for the entertainment of the Marines on duty; our choice. There were some real finds, too. As they searched us one at a time, they yelled out what they had found.

"You puke," the Marine would start yelling, "You want this picture of a naked whore sent home to your momma? How about this rubber, you want your old man to use it on your momma? No … shit …, he should have used one before you were born, you miserable excuse of a man."

"No, sir!" the recruit would reply. And so it continued on down the line. After each Marine was searched and questioned, the box of clothes, pictures, and other items was sealed and left in the cubicle.

Eventually the Marines on duty had a whole slew of pictures and other material that could not be sent home to momma. They looked at them and laughed, as we stood naked at attention. Sometimes it was hard to keep from laughing, too, as they were quite funny at times, and they would have to yell and scream at us to get back to attention. Finally the magic hour came and we were taken, ten at a time, to the shower. When we returned, a supply Marine was waiting with shower shoes, green utility pants, yellow sweat shirt, and utility cover. He would glance at each man and pick a size for him. Finally we were able to dress and fall back to attention with our utility cover tucked in the waistband of our trousers, until the others were finished with their showers and clothing. It was the first time we learned about not wearing any hat (cover) indoors. The Marines called it being uncovered. It was still dark and I was still holding out hope for a few hours sleep. But then SSgt. V came into the room.

He was the first Marine with a Smokey Bear cover I had seen since the ones we saw when we had first arrived in San Diego, and he could wear it inside. This was the only cover that could be worn indoors. He was our real drill instructor, one of three we would have for the next seven weeks. He wasted no time insulting us as a group and had us double-time outside to stand on the yellow footprints again. He was yelling at us to put our utility covers on our heads because we were outside now. He made us lock arms, four at a time, and attempted to march us in four columns away from the receiving building. He soon gave up, and we walked slowly, arm in arm, to our destination.

I was still holding out hope of some sleep, but it turned out that our march was to the mess hall.

We went inside single file, picking up metal trays and having everyone on duty yelling at us to take our covers off as we went inside. They gave us no choice about what to eat for breakfast, and we were told to eat everything that was given. We went through the sit-down drill again and finally ate. Afterwards our trays were inspected for leftover food, and we hustled outside, putting our covers back on.

After breakfast and for the next few days we spent most of our time being issued clothes, toiletries, gear, padlocks, M-14 rifles, and the like. Later that first day we were joined by our second drill instructor, Sgt. B.

I took an instant dislike to him, preferring SSgt. V. The new sergeant was meaner and called us names more often. He was real short with a huge Napoleon complex. We never did get to sleep until nine o'clock the next night so it was a very long first day. That night we picked our bunks, and my buddy Gregg and I took the first bunk on the left past the door, or hatch, as it would be known from then on. I took the top and he took the bottom. Before we turned in we had a group shower and shave. We all shaved even though the majority had no whiskers. Afterward we returned to our Quonset hut. The hut was a WWII era half circle metal building housing a maximum of twenty recruits, which is what we had in our squad. We were the first squad of four; therefore we were closest to the drill instructors' hut.

Just before taps, Sgt. B (we called him Igor) came in and told us all that when we heard reveille in the morning to be ready to go to formation by the time the bugle stopped playing. He told me, as occupier of the top first bunk on the left, that I had to open or close the hatch on his command. He told Greg to turn the lights on or off. His last words were, "You will sleep," before he moved on to the next hut. SSgt. V had disappeared, no doubt because he had been with us since early morning, and we didn't see him until the next day.

Taps sounded and from outside on the company road Sgt. B yelled, "Platoon 3044, lights off, hatches closed."

I closed the hatch and Greg shut off the lights and everyone was quiet. It didn't take long to fall asleep, and we slept soundly; too soundly.

The next thing I heard was reveille, loud and clear. It took a few moments to realize that it was morning because it was still dark outside. I slowly came awake and, as the bugle stopped, I heard the unmistakable sound of Sgt. B yelling from the company road.

"Platoon 3044, lights on, hatches open," he roared.

I didn't have time to think about my door duty before Sgt. B burst through the hatch, flipped on the light switch and came directly at me, grabbing me by the arms and throwing me to the floor.

"When I say lights on, hatches open, I mean NOW," he bellowed. By then everybody was up and standing at attention. "Get dressed! Formation in two minutes!"

That afternoon we met our third and final drill instructor, Gsgt. VV, and I liked him instantly even though he was calling us every name under the sun. Gsgt. VV was our platoon commander, and he would become the father figure I always wanted. Whenever we made eye contact I felt we had a special connection. I can't explain it other than it felt like he should have been my father. I know that sounds weird, but that's how I felt, and after the end of our seven weeks, I would have followed him into hell. So would every other recruit.

I won't spend a lot of time on the first three weeks of boot camp other to say that it was the tearing-down phase. It was the learning to march phase, and it was the don't run home to momma or you go to jail phase, and it was the learning the Marine Corps way phase. We had good days and bad days and days we wished we were dead. We walked around with wrinkled utilities with the top button buttoned, or red shorts, or yellow sweatshirts, and they called us canaries, girls, ladies, and worse. By inspection the third week, our platoon was top platoon in our series of four, and our reward was cleaning the post rather than mess duty, which the other three platoons had to face. We also were allowed to blouse our trousers exposing our black boots. Now this doesn't seem like a big deal, but to Marine recruits it meant you were starting the "We Build Marines" phase of boot camp.

During that week I had my broken tooth extracted, and it became infected the next day. My face swelled up to the size of a melon, and Sgt. B was beside himself. He thought someone beat me up. They took me to the dental clinic and to the hospital from there. I was in a hospital bed for three days and two nights. I was afraid I would be left behind and begged the doctor to let me get back to my platoon. He gave in and let me go. I double-timed to the platoon drill instructors' hut and found the platoon gone, still on grounds duty. Gsgt. VV and SSgt. V were inside.

I came to attention outside the hut and pounded as hard as I could three times on the hatch. Gsgt. VV looked up, and then SSgt. V looked up.

SSgt. V said," Speak!"

"Sir," I said loudly, "the private wants permission to speak to the drill instructor, sir."

"Enter," SSgt. V said.

I came inside and took off my cover and snapped to attention again.

This time it was Gsgt. VV who spoke. "You better have something good to say, private." He never called me names.

"Sir," I replied, "the private wishes to continue with the platoon, sir." And then with a lapse in military etiquette, I continued, "Please don't send me back a week." I did so without starting with "sir" or ending with "sir," and I knew immediately that I screwed up. For some reason they let it slide, and they looked at each other. I think now they realized that they had established a bond in the platoon, because they told me to go to my squad hut and make sure all was clean until the platoon returned. I was so happy I could kiss them. I said, "Sir, yes, sir," about faced and left.

The rest of that week we refined our drill, took history classes, and finished up with pugil sticks, where broom handles with padded ends served as bayonets. We all thought this would be a fun time and it was for most. We wore football helmets for safety and went about our training. I excelled at the basic bayonet drills, but on the last afternoon we matched up against another platoon for three minutes of all out battle, one pair at a time. We lined up in two long lines at random, and I was somewhere in the middle. As I looked at the enemy platoon lined up some fifteen feet away, I could only see one big guy to be concerned about. As each of the three-minute battles went on, the lines moved up to the battle ring. After about twenty minutes it became apparent that I was the same number in line as the big guy across the way.

I jokingly tried to see if any of my platoon mates wanted to move up or back a notch, and when they all counted back to themselves, they realized I had the brute.

"Why me?" I thought, " I just got out of the hospital a couple of days ago."

I thought maybe Sgt. B would remember my swollen face from last week and let me slide, but no such luck. We reached our time and the big guy and I put our helmets on and took up the position.

It didn't look as bad as it was because we were both about six foot, four inches in height; only problem was he weighed a good 250 pounds and I weighed 144. At the command to fight my long reach and quickness allowed me the first straight blow to the helmet, which pissed off my opponent, and he commenced to beat the hell out of me for two minutes and fifty-eight seconds. Thank God we had helmets; my face came out of it okay.

That weekend we prepared for the M-14 rifle qualifying range by cleaning our rifles, breaking them down and cleaning them again. On Sunday afternoon we took a break to go to the outside wash racks with our red shorts and buckets to wash our clothes. While we were doing that Gregg bumped my arm to get my attention and nodded toward SSgt. V and another Marine in khakis with a barracks cover instead of a Smokey Bear cover. On closer examination we saw that it was our old friend from high school, Hank, who was ready to deploy to Vietnam. He explained his situation to SSgt. V who let him come over and talk to us. Hank was a lance corporal E-3 and had joined a year before. He came over and we shook hands and hugged. He said SSgt. V had only given him two minutes to talk and then he had to go because he was in a restricted area. I had written Hank a few weeks earlier to tell him our platoon number and that is how he had found us. It was so great seeing him, and Gregg and I felt very proud to have him take the time to see us.

We wished him luck in Vietnam, and when SSgt. V was turned away, he snapped two pictures of us with our buckets. Hank said his goodbyes and walked back over to SSgt. V and shook hands with him. It looked like the sarge wished Hank luck as well.

Next morning we left for Camp Pendleton on buses to spend ten days at the rifle range. As I said before, our platoon was a few days past seven weeks in boot camp. Those of you, who know better, you know that Marine Corps boot camp is and was normally thirteen weeks. In September of 1967 they were sending more and more troops to Vietnam, and as the build-up continued they needed bodies fast. Thus our training was cut short. The normal two weeks for snapping in and live fire was cut to ten or eleven days.

We stayed in modern two story concrete barracks with nice toilet facilities and warm squad bay. The drill instructors had their glass enclosed office in the middle, and they spent most of their time at night playing fast draw with their real six-guns and holsters like it was the old west.

Snapping in was a bitch. For the uninitiated, it is the process of learning the basic positions of fire: sitting, prone, standing, et cetera. It doesn't seem like a big deal, but for those of us who went through it, we still feel the pain. Live fire was really neat. I for one had never fired a rifle before, and the few days we spent doping our rifles was an enjoyable experience. Once you knew how many "clicks" up or down, right or left to put on your sights, it was just a matter of holding steady and squeezing the trigger. Easier said than done.

Once again, since our platoon had taken some more honors, we were picked to carry ammo when we were not shooting instead of working the target pits.

On Thursday of that week we had our trial rifle qualification. The majority of us did well, but we were pressing to have 100% qualification. There were five different shooting positions and distances, for a total of 50 rounds. Each round had a maximum award of five points for an inner circle bull's-eye, four for the next outer, then three and two. If you missed the target, it was zero, or Maggie's Drawers, which was the red flag they waved from the pit. Qualifying meant you had to score 190 or above, and the majority of us did it in the trial. The drill instructors now knew who they had to help tomorrow to see if all would qualify. I shot 207.

The morning came, and we all made sure we had the right dope written down for the various distances to use on our rifle sights, and we headed to the range.

"Ready on the left, ready on the right, ready on the firing line, commence firing."

I scored a 214, sharpshooter, as did most in the platoon. 220 and above was "expert" and ten guys made it. The rest, with the exception of two men, all qualified marksman. It was disappointing not to have a 100% qualifying, and those two felt bad, but we did better than the other three platoons and took the streamer for the rifle range to add to the others on our platoon flag.

When we returned to MCRD we wore starched utilities for the first time with our top shirt buttons undone, and when we marched now, we were tight and sharp. The last two weeks of boot camp consisted of another test (which I think I aced), a movie, a football game on post, and countless drills to get ready for final inspection. Our platoon took more of those honors, and the day of final inspection was no different. The regiment commander went down the row of each squad, taking the rifle and inspecting it. At times he would ask some men questions about Marine history and rifle nomenclature, trying to trip them up. I was the second in line of my squad, tallest to the front, and as such I was the first to get questions.

The officer stood right in front of me with Gsgt. VV in front of the squad leader and grabbed my rifle looking it over. He began asking me names of the rifle parts, Naval ranks, Marine history, the military code of justice, and he couldn't stump me. He turned to Gsgt. VV and said, "Very good, sergeant."

He returned my rifle, did a right face, took one step and stood in front of the next guy. Gsgt. VV followed him, and as he turned, he was looking right at my face. I had to try hard to keep a straight face. I was so glad I did well for him, the platoon, and me. I think he may have had a slight smile on his face before moving on. We won final inspection and graduated Honor Platoon on 4 October 1967. They called us Marines for the first time.

We had the afternoon off with base liberty, and I was surprised to see my older cousin Marla in the crowd. She was married to a Marine sergeant, and my mother had written her to tell her when we were to graduate. Most of the guys had no one on hand because in those days airfares were very high for working class families, and most of us came from poor families. We had a great afternoon, eating ice cream and hamburgers mostly, and I really appreciated her coming.

That night was the first time the drill instructors treated us like human beings. We actually sat around and bullshitted with Igor (Sgt. B) and found him to be a pretty good guy. After a good night's sleep and an early breakfast, we gathered our things and waited on the company road for our MOS (Military Occupational Specialty) assignments and buses to take us to Camp Pendleton and ITR (Infantry Training Regiment).

Shortly Gsgt. VV, SSgt. V, and Sgt. B, showed up and said a little speech each as we all cheered at what each said. Then they started reading off the MOS assignments. I knew most of us would be infantry, but I was hoping my test scores would help me get something safer. Since we did everything alphabetically, I didn't have to wait long.

"0300, 0300, 0300," the sergeant read off the code for infantry, and when they called my name they said, "0800, artillery." I was pleased. It wasn't, 0100 office worker, as I had hoped, but it wasn't infantry either.

It turned out that my buddies Gregg and Mike were assigned 0300 infantry.

Within an hour the buses arrived. All non-infantry Marines got on one bus, and the 0300s got on the others. I never saw Gsgt. VV, or SSgt. V, or Sgt. B again. With the exception of Gregg and Mike and two others, I never saw any one from my platoon again.

ITR (Infantry Training Regiment)

After arriving at Camp Pendleton, our bus took us to the San Onofre part of the camp. We thought we would go to the nice two story barracks like we had at the rifle range, but we had wood and canvas tents instead, with canvas cots. All those that had made PFC out of boot camp became squad leaders, and they wasted no time getting us into squads and platoons. Everyone in my ITR company was something other than infantry, but being Marines first we had to take a scaled down version of M-60 machine gun training, M-79 grenade launcher, flame thrower, mortar, and hand grenade training, as well as basic combat maneuvers in a platoon situation.

We all had a chance to fire those weapons and throw a live grenade, but the real highlight was that we had more company area free time. We were not allowed base liberty, but after evening chow and weekends, our time was our own. Lots of letter writing and sleeping in. Some of the black Marines formed little squad formations for fun and would march around together like a drill team in a parade back home. Most of us thought they were nuts, but I think they enjoyed it.

The real highlight for me was the end of the third week when volunteers were sought for duty at the San Onofre Beach Canteen. This was a little hamburger stand/restaurant on Camp property right on the beach, and was for Marine personnel only. Since I had nothing else to do and had fryer cook experience, I decided to volunteer. Smart move on my part.

The beach was great, and the little canteen was a great place to work. All the food (hamburgers and fries) you could eat and lots of time to take a dip in the ocean. It was a great two days, and I must have made a thousand hamburgers for all the camp Marines that came to swim and sunbathe.

Our final week of ITR was nothing extraordinary, and that Friday they let us go to an open-air theater. We sat outside on log benches in about ten rows. The movie was nothing special as I remember, but what happened afterward was devastating for me. Somewhere, sometime, between the tent and the movie, I lost my wallet.

We had just been paid, and we all had $99.00 cash for the month of October. My pay, my ID card, and ticket home for 30 days leave starting Monday – everything was missing!

I couldn't believe it. I told my platoon sergeant, and all day Saturday we searched for the wallet, hoping it would be returned. It wasn't, and I was afraid I would not be able to go home, but on Sunday the duty officer took me to the main gate and had the MPs photograph me and issue me a new ID card. Then they contacted the airlines and made arrangements for a replacement ticket. Lastly I got an emergency loan of $50.00 against my November pay and was able to get home.

Over two months later when I was in staging battalion, my wallet was returned to me, with only the ID card inside. It was found by a dumpster somewhere on post and returned to the MPs who tracked me down. It was now apparent that someone either took it from my back pocket or found it and took the money. Either way I felt bad for the guy who did it. Stealing from another Marine was just unthinkable to me. Stealing leave money from any Marine who may be dead in a few months seemed just a dirty shame. They always say that ten percent of any group causes a hundred percent of the crime and bad deeds, and as much as I wanted to think that all Marines were brothers, there was still that ten percent who weren't in spite of Marine Corps ethical and moral standards.

THIRTY DAYS HOME

When I got to the airport in LA I felt very proud wearing my uniform even though everyone knew I was just out of boot camp. Just my National Defense Ribbon and Sharpshooters Badge on my chest. I was in awe of the Vietnam Veterans who were all over the airport as well. I didn't talk to them and neither did any one else. There were lots of hippies and harikrishna types around chanting peace and goodwill. We just had to ignore them and enjoy the occasional reunion of parents and Vietnam Veteran sons in the airport lobby. Mostly we just sat and waited for our flight.

When I got off the plane in Seattle, I was met by my mom and step dad and taken the short five-mile ride home. Some of the neighbors came by to wish me well, but I wanted to drive my car and see my friends. The next thirty days were bittersweet as I broke up with my current girlfriend and started a friendship with one of Greg's girlfriends. He was okay with that, and this new girl and I got pretty close by the time Thanksgiving rolled around. I couldn't go many places or do much because I was broke. The $50.00 didn't last long and my parents were pretty tight. My mom slipped me a few bucks to keep me in gas money.

Thanksgiving was great. I always enjoyed seeing my relatives in Port Orchard on the west side of Puget Sound across from Seattle. The food was good, my family was happy, and life couldn't better. Of course within a few days reality came screaming back, hitting me hard the day before I was to return to California. That queasy stomach, that deep sense of fear was returning, and I hated it. I wished I was stronger, but I could only try to hide my true feelings and self-doubt.

When it was finally time to go to the airport, there were tears from all my family and friends. As I boarded the southbound 707, I felt very alone. I reached my seat and started thinking of my situation.

I was thinking of what one of my friends had told me earlier in the week about all the macho athletic types in high school that bragged about their medical deferments for football and baseball injuries, but were still able to go to college and play, and in some cases enter the major leagues.

Most people don't realize that there were only two NFL players that were Vietnam Veterans and only one Major League Baseball player. Years later Vietnam Veterans would be maligned as poor kids of average abilities and intelligence. I'm here to tell you they did more heroic things than any two-bit athlete with a deferment ever did, and many like myself became college graduates, and most became decent citizens and family men. I'm proud of my military brothers and sisters, especially those who overcame their poor roots and succeeded in civilian life.

ARTILLERY SCHOOL

It was three days after Thanksgiving, 1967, when my Uncle Phil met me at Los Angeles International Airport. He had been in LA for business, and we were going to dinner before he would take me back to Camp Pendleton. All through dinner I had uneasiness in my stomach because I knew that I would be leaving for Vietnam in several weeks and might never see my family again. For the most part, I knew the odds were in my favor, and I never really thought I would die in war, but from time to time the notion would sneak into on my consciousness and briefly scare me. This was one of those times.

After dinner, Uncle Phil took me down to Camp Pendleton, and I checked in at the main gate. We said our goodbyes and as my uncle left, I wondered if this would be the last time I saw any of my family. The MPs called for a van, and I was transferred a short distance to a transit barracks.

It was late and the sleeping bay was already dark when the watch NCO gave me my two sheets, a blanket, pillowcase and pillow. I searched for an empty bunk amid the snoring of a dozen or so transits and was fortunate to find one with both top and bottom empty. I unrolled the mattress and put the case on the pillow. Pushing my sea bag under the bottom bunk, I left the sheets still folded under the pillow and lay down without trying to make the bed. I just lay there fully clothed staring at the wire springs of the bunk above.

I guess I spent an hour or so re-living my life to that point and concluded that it hadn't been too good so far. There were so many things I wanted to do and experience, and now I was on my way to a war. Part of me was excited to start artillery school; part of me wished I wasn't going. Part of me was looking forward to coming to grips with my personal fears and returning home a Vietnam Veteran; part of me wished I could start fulfilling my wishes and goals without the threat of war. Of course I missed my family and my friends. I wondered what my old girlfriend was doing at that moment. She was a high school senior now and had another new boyfriend and was probably very happy in her situation. I was not. I was feeling bad, very sorry for myself. I hated feeling that way, but as I lay there in that dark squad bay with the other boys snoring around me, I just couldn't help it. I may have even cried a little. Big bad Marine!

The next day we had an informal formation, and our orders were collected. I spent that day in the transit barracks with many other guys waiting for new orders. More boys came every hour, two or three at a time. We were all waiting to be transferred to a Schools battalion that would be our MOS (Military Occupational Specialty) training before leaving for Vietnam. It was boring as hell that day with nothing to do. The only distraction was when the lunch truck came by.

Since there wasn't an operating chow hall nearby, none of us had had breakfast, and I didn't have much money left over from leave so I could only get a candy bar, doughnut, and a soft drink. Finally, late in the afternoon my name was called, and along with about a dozen other Marines, I left in a truck to another part of the base. We drove for some thirty minutes and were checked into another temporary barracks. The Cpl. in charge got an ear full of how hungry we all were, and he called the mess hall to ask them to hold the doors open another ten minutes so we could get over there. We double-timed. We arrived at the mess hall, and didn't waste any time, eating quickly and stuffing extra food in our pockets before we left.

I can't remember much about any of the guys I was with during this time. They were just guys like me. Lonely, young, and deep down inside we were all scared.

The next morning it was like being back in boot camp. The corporal came by at six with reveille and we had to make our bunks, shave, shower, and clean the barracks before we could go to chow. I'm sure I ate a big breakfast that morning. When we returned to the barracks we had morning formation, and different NCOs came by to pick work parties from our ranks. We were still waiting for enough men to return from leave after their ITR training to form our Schools battalion. There were only about twenty of us that morning. I was among those picked to go to a deserted bakery building to clean it prior to its re-opening. A van took us there and dropped us off.

We mopped, swept, and washed windows, pots and pans. It was not too hard because the building had been closed for a long time. Mostly just dust on everything. There was a mess hall next to the bakery so we walked over for lunch. In the afternoon there wasn't much left to do so when we were done we just sat around and bull-shitted with the corporal until the van returned to take us back to the barracks.

There was an immediate change in things when we got back as there were now twice as many Marines in our squad bay. New guys had been arriving all day long. Our Schools battalion would commence in a few days.

The next morning I was assigned to a work party that was formed to make a vacant building into a party room. Seems that a Master Gunnery Sgt. was retiring after thirty years, and we cleaned and mopped and swept once again. Tables were set up with linen table clothes, and little Marine Corps and American flags were placed in the center of each table. Towards the end of the afternoon the Master Gsgt. in question came by to look at the set-up. We all thought he would be a hard case, but he turned out to be warm and appreciative. He had many battle ribbons on his chest, from WWII and

Korea: purple hearts, bronze and silver stars. He was short and stocky, and later I always wished that I had remembered his name because I'm sure he was a hero at Tarawa or Guadalcanal or some other such place.

The next day we had over a hundred men in formation, and I was not picked for a work party since I had gone the previous two days. Those of us that stayed at the barracks spent the morning policing the grounds and cleaning the squad bay. After lunch we just sat around until the duty NCO tossed us a basketball. Every barracks had at least one basketball hoop and backboard as part of the cement grinder (the place we marched) in front of the entrance. We took turns playing four on four all afternoon. I was terrible. Even though I was 6 feet 4 inches tall, I had never played much basketball. Some of the boys were really good, and before the afternoon was over most of us non-basketball types had rudimentary training in setting screens and blocking out for rebounds. We also learned who to pass the ball to for a shot.

After evening chow we got the word that we would be leaving in the morning for our different schools. We were all glad it was finally happening, although I would miss the basketball. In that one afternoon I had been hooked and wanted to play more in the future. As I was soon to find out, basketball would continue for a while.

The next morning we split into groups of the same MOS, and my group, 0844 Fire Direction Control, consisted of about two dozen Marines. Over the last few days I had founds guys with my same MOS as that was the first question any of us asked each other when we first met. So, I knew some of the guys already, two Marines in particular; Dave was from Indiana and the other from Oklahoma, but I can't remember his name now. We became good friends and were inseparable during the next month.

It was December now, and as we got our gear together we were glad we only had to march a short distance to our FDC barracks. The barracks was a two story wood structure with two squad bays on each floor. In the center of the building were the barracks' office and staircase, and out front was a 50x100 foot concrete grinder we used for formations; it just happened to have a basketball hoop and backstop. I was pleased. The lower right squad bay was for FDC, 0844 only, and the other three were for 0811, the canon cockers, or guys on the guns. There obviously were more men needed to shoot the howitzers than were needed to do the math that made them hit the target.

From the first my new classmates were different than the average Marine I met in boot camp and ITR. We all seemed a little more mature and educated, and it was clear that they were very selective in choosing us for our math skills. We got our bunks chosen and squared away and then went to lunch. The afternoon was free and spent playing basketball. Little by little my game improved.

Our classroom the next morning was just a short walk, and it actually felt good to be in a classroom with twenty people again. We didn't waste any time, and each day we learned more and more, and actually it was so interesting to see how artillery math worked that the two weeks passed by in a flash. We constantly took quizzes and reviewed things guys had trouble with. Try as I may, I could not out-do this one Marine. His test and quiz score averaged 96 and mine was 95 after two weeks. They kept a public log of everyone's place in class, and I would be number two at the beginning and number two at the end. The good news was that no one was below an 80 average.

After that first two weeks we had our first real liberty as Marines. We all had civilian clothes with us now, and we tried to dress like we weren't Marines. Most of us wore our military black oxford shoes and our haircuts were so short that everyone could tell we were military. The reason we wished we didn't look so conspicuous was two-fold. First all, at that time, the civilian guys had long hair and the girls had long hair, and the girls liked guys with long hair; so finding a girl that would give you the time of day was impossible. Second, the younger part of the nation was well into the protest movement now, and we were at times subjected to insults and "looks" as we made our way around in the civilian world.

It was a shame that those things happened, but they were less likely to happen in Southern California where the military was a large part of the community. Basically, we had two main liberty options at Camp Pendleton: head north to Disneyland or south to Tijuana. Most of my class headed north.

It was my second time to Disneyland as the first was in 1958 when I was eleven. My mom had acquired leftover tickets from co-workers, and we had caught a ride with a friend who was going home to see her parents in California and needed extra gas money.

I loved Disneyland the second time as much as the first time and had a ball. No matter that the girls didn't talk to us; no one did. It was like we had the plague or something, but we had a good time together. Three of my classmates and I rented a motel room across the street from Disneyland, and we spent all day Saturday there. We were there early, and it was one of the few places that actually had a reduced fee for military. We had money and it was nice to be able to get whatever food you wanted without parents telling you no. We rode the rides, ate a lot of food, watched the girls, and had a marvelous time even though no one thanked us for our service. Sunday morning we had a big breakfast at a Denny's nearby and returned to Oceanside where we hung around until after dark before heading back to the School barracks. That night the guys from Tijuana would come rolling in drunk and sore from tattoos that they got on various parts of their bodies, mostly upper arms. That next morning they were easy to spot and easy targets for a slap or punch on their sore arms. One fellow in particular had his arm swell up so bad it became infected and he had to go to the hospital. He was reprimanded and used as an example of why one should stay out of Mexico. He was dropped from our class, and rumor had it that he was going to the infantry, but that was just rumor. He showed up in the class behind us the following week.

The third week of class was exciting because we had our first visit to the field where we watched the 0844 and 0811 classes ahead of us do their fire missions in real time with real shells and artillery. We would do the same all next week so we had something to look forward to. That weekend there was no liberty so we stayed on base and played a lot of basketball.

Saturday night the outdoor theater in the Schools area had a great war movie playing: “The Dirty Dozen.” It starred every Hollywood badass at the time and was one of the best war movies made in the sixties. I can’t tell you how much fun it was watching that movie with a hundred Marines laughing, shouting, cheering the on-screen exploits, and having just such a wonderful time with the guys. It was the first time since boot camp that I felt a brotherhood with my School Marines, a process that would return over and over again as I moved through my different Vietnam assignments. That night and that movie were unforgettable.

The following week was the week before Christmas, and we spent most of the time in the field doing live fire. The artillery firing range was in a remote spot, a valley east of the main part of the base. Our FDC (Fire Direction Center) was on a hill and the six guns were down the hill and to the left a few hundred meters. We could see the guns from our FDC. The target area was two miles away in the valley below us. There were a few 55-

gallon drums gathered close together to give us a visual target.

Everyone got a chance to do the chart and do the computing and watch the rounds hit. Every once in while the rounds would hit way off target which meant the FDC screwed up, and every once in a while one or two of the six rounds would be way off target which meant the individual gun crew screwed up.

Our lunch was catered by the mess hall, so we had hot food on those cold December days. After that week our confidence grew, and we were ready to go on to final exams and graduation.

Christmas that year (1967) was on a Monday, and it was like the Camp was deserted. We had liberty, but it was near the end of the month and everyone was broke so most of us stayed on base. On Saturday my two buds and I went to Oceanside for hamburgers, and while we were there we decided to get a picture taken in dress blues, at one of the many photo studios that lined the main drag. The photographer asked us what rank we wanted to have on the dress blues, and we said we were privates.

He said, "Look, you guys are at least going to be PFC's in Vietnam, and if you get killed you will want to have a nice picture with rank and medals for your family to remember you by."

The bluntness of his words*, if you get killed*, shook me a little, but even though I didn't rate them I agreed to PFC stripes, the Vietnam campaign ribbons and a gold shoulder braid, although I never knew what it represented. The picture was taken and processed within an hour. I did feel better when I paid to have it sent home to my parents. I thought that it looked good enough to remember me by.

The next two days, Christmas Eve and Christmas, were very boring. I remember having no lunch as most of the cooks got those days off, and only a small crew of cooks made breakfast and dinner. I walked around the schools area in the afternoon and over to the main road where the PX and gas station were. They closed early, and I sat on a bench watching lifer Marines and their families' drive by heading to Christmas get-togethers. It was my worst Christmas. The only one without a tree and lights and at least friends to be with. I never felt so alone as I did those two days. I tried to call my girlfriend and parents but couldn't get through to them. No cell phones back then. I was eager for my last week of class to start.

Tuesday of that last week started with a review of everything we had learned, and the review continued until Friday afternoon when we took our final exam. This was my last chance to be number one, and I knew I did very, very, well on it. That weekend we had liberty again, and one of the guys had a San Diego newspaper that advertised a teenage dance on Saturday December 30th. We got paid Friday, the day of our final test, so my buddies and I caught a bus to San Diego and shared a downtown hotel room a few blocks from where the dance was to be held. We were bored after breakfast Saturday and went to the movies twice that afternoon while waiting for the seven o'clock start of the dance.

After dinner we got to the dance early, as we had nothing else to do. We paid our money, got our hand stamped, and found a corner of the ballroom to stake out as our own. We sat there and waited for the girls to show up. Needless to say lots of girls came, but they almost all had dates, and those that didn't had an over-supply of longer-haired guys to pick from. The dance was fun, and it was bittersweet looking at the girls because they were nice to look at, but none us even tried asking for a dance. It was like we were invisible; no one even talked to us. It would be Disneyland for us tomorrow, and we couldn't wait until the first bus left for Anaheim the next morning. Once again Mickey Mouse and Donald Duck saved our Sunday and Monday New Year.

We had finished school, so on the second of January 1968, we had a graduation ceremony. The top five of us were singled out as high achievers and the number one Marine and I were further singled out as acing the final test. He was promoted to PFC and the rest of us were not. They promoted everyone in boot camp that shot expert on the firing range, but here, even though I aced the final, they only acknowledged the top average guy. I lost out by percentage points. It was one of the few times I lost respect for the Corps. I felt they only associated intelligence with the officer corps, but I was to learn different in Vietnam. They mailed our diplomas home to our parents.

STAGING BATTLION

The next morning we boarded buses and drove out to some remote spot on the base. It was a narrow valley between two treeless hills. Now it was January and even though it was Southern California, it was still cold at night. We were surprised to find that we were billeted in large canvas tents with kerosene stoves in the center instead of a nice heated barracks. We were quickly formed into rifle companies, platoons, and squads. One platoon to each big tent. I found myself with only one fellow classmate from school. We had canvas cots instead of bunks, and the first night was pretty cold.

Waking up the next morning, there was little warmth from the stove, and we dressed without delay for morning chow. Everyone had their field jackets on, of course, and we marched to the mess hall, ate breakfast, but never returned to the tents. As the morning wore on the sun came out and we were getting too hot for jackets. By the time we were issued all of our gear, some guys asked if we were going back to the tents at lunch so we could leave our jackets and the new gear. The sergeants said no, and it was our first lesson, albeit unfair, about taking only what you are sure you would need for the job at hand. In Vietnam it would be important to only take what was necessary for that patrol or operational deployment.

The last piece of equipment issued that afternoon was an M-16. The M-16 was much different from the M-14 we had in boot camp. There was no wood stock and it had plastic parts. It was lighter than the M-14 and that was a good thing. We had heard rumors that it jammed easier in combat so we all paid close attention to the cleaning and care instructions.

That night it was very cold and the next morning dawned clear. None of us wore our field jackets to breakfast, thinking we would not return to the tents, so we froze on the way to the mess hall. We were wrong and returned to get only the gear we would need for that morning. We continued to freeze until about 10 am when the sun warmed the air. For the next two weeks we were taught all there was to know about fighting in Vietnam, including rifle company procedures, booby-traps, and tunnels; we even had a fake village to train in. In retrospect it wasn't very realistic. Our instructors were all Vietnam veterans just back from the war. Even though a lot of us would not be in the infantry, we would all have to know the training just in case we had to be emergency infantrymen. It had happened all too often in past wars. Most of the time the instructors would tell us what to take for the morning and afternoon, and we would return to the tents frequently to drop off field jackets or other equipment and take other things back out with us.

One of the last days of Staging Battalion started this way, and we wore our field jackets in the morning and returned for lunch, leaving the jackets at camp for the afternoon training session. When the afternoon session was completed, we marched to the mess hall for dinner and thought we were going back to camp for a normal evening. Wrong, so wrong! To our displeasure we found that we were not going back to the tents, but marched out into the hills where we took up defensive positions; three men to a hole with at least one man awake all night. It was too damned cold to sleep, and without our field jackets we froze all night long. I never spent a longer or colder night outside in my whole life. It was to teach us that even though we were going to a warm weather war, earlier Marines suffered in very cold conditions in Korea and WWII. When morning finally came, they marched us back to the tents where we got warm by the kerosene stove and put on our jackets before going to breakfast.

That day our training ended with a pep talk by the battalion commander. He told us tomorrow we would be bused to an Air Force base in San Bernardino where we would board a flight to the Western Pacific. We had the rest of the day off and it was spent writing letters. Again I cannot remember much about any one person from those three weeks of training, except the faces of artillery school classmates that I saw on occasion. I can only guess that knowing I would not be with anyone of them in Vietnam, there was no use making any good relationships. Also my camera was locked in my footlocker the whole time, so no pictures were taken of that time.

FLYING THE FRIENDLY SKIES OF CONTINENTAL

The day of our departure was bright and sunny. We boarded buses for the trip north to San Bernardino, and when we reached the Air Force base, they took us into a huge square building by the airstrip. It was some sort of terminal or station of departure building, but inside was a large open area with only a few benches, high ceilings, and a small store and snack bar. It seemed like it may have been a hanger at one time. Most of us sat on our sea-bags on the floor and waited and waited. We all assumed that we would fly to Vietnam on an Air Force plane of some type, so we were surprised to see a Continental Boeing 320 commercial airliner pull up to the terminal late in the afternoon. They checked our sea bags, and we boarded the jet. Since I was taller than most, I got to sit in the first row in front of the forward bulkhead next to a lieutenant and another tall enlisted man. When I saw the pretty flight attendants helping us to our seats, I was really surprised. The captain came on the intercom and told us we would be flying to Honolulu airport where we would lay over for a couple of hours. We all were excited because none of us had even been to Hawaii before.

The flight went well with great food and good company, and the flight attendants were very good at keeping our morale high. I was really enjoying the trip and didn't give much thought to our final destination. When we arrived at Honolulu airport we were confined to the end of one terminal building wing with only limited windows and bathrooms. No snack bar, no seats, no civilians, or anything else but the rope barriers. For two hours we stood around like cattle, finally re-boarding the same plane. The flight crew was different, and it was getting dark as we took flight again. We learned that our next stop was at the government refueling station on Wake Island. That precipitated thoughts of WWII, and I remembered the boot camp history classes we had about Wake Island and the eventual surrender to Japanese forces when it was clear no help would be forthcoming.

We landed on Wake Island around midnight. It was very dark with only a small terminal and few lights outside. We were not allowed in the terminal, but were told we could walk over to the beach about 200 yards away while they refueled the plane. It was very windy with a light rain and very dark. I remember huge bulkhead boulders on the beach with the waves crashing against the rocks in the pitch black. Shortly we were called back and re-boarded the plane. We had been awake for more then twenty hours now, so most everyone slept the final leg to Okinawa.

The morning found us landing on a cloudy day at Kadena AFB, Okinawa. We said goodbye to the Continental crew, got our sea bags, and boarded buses for the short ride to a Marine facility where we were assigned to new concrete barracks with modern toilets, urinals, sinks and showers. After chow, the officers let us sleep the rest of the day. At night some guys asked about liberty, but we were told there would be none as we could pack up and leave for Vietnam at any time.

Next morning we lounged around our bunks after breakfast, and then two other FDC artillery guys and I walked around the outside of the barracks. One of the guys was with me in artillery school, although I don't remember his name now, and he and I had our picture taken in front of an old abandoned Ford station wagon with graffiti written all over it.

While we were outside, we noticed a supply building with a garage sized door open and various Marines milling around. Seems as though they had surplus jungle utility shirts and pants and were giving them away. The clothes were in an awful state. One Marine asked where these came from, and we were told that these clothes were taken from wounded and dead Marines. These were the good leftovers and the rest were burned. This dimmed our enthusiasm for the free jungle utilities, but I found an unusual short sleeve shirt that I still have today.

After lunch we were told to stand by inside, ready to leave at a moment's notice. The call came before evening chow, and we boarded buses for the airbase. We arrived at the same Kadena AFB terminal we had been at the day before and spent some time milling around as a group. I watched as Air Force pilots in full flight gear, and of every officer rank, came and went. I never saw so many officers; it was a good thing we were inside where we didn't have to salute. Finally we were told to saddle up, and we boarded another Continental airplane, which shocked us again, because we knew our next stop was DaNang, Vietnam, and the war. The flight attendants were great again, and after about an hour on the plane we were told to de-plane, but were not given a reason. We heard a rumor that the airfield at DaNang was taking incoming rocket fire. We were returned to the Marine barracks, but slept with our clothes on. The next morning, after breakfast, we headed back to Kadena.

We found our same areas on the terminal floor and settled in for another wait. Late in the afternoon we got the call, and we lined up to board the plane only to be stopped a short time later. We returned to the terminal floor, but our sea bags stayed on the plane. Once again the rumors were flying about attacks on the airbase at DaNang. How true they were. We continued watching the

Air Force pilots come and go. We slept fitfully and sometime in the early dark morning we awoke and lined up to board the Continental Boeing 320 for the third time in two days. We were tired and hungry, but the flight attendants were fresh and beautiful and at the top of their morale game. We quickly became airborne, were served an in-flight breakfast, and the flight attendants got us happy and smiling again. The girls were really beautiful and young, but still a few years older then most of us. They were wonderful.

The sun rose as we neared Vietnam; it was shining brightly with only a few clouds. The pilot came on the intercom and told us that DaNang had taken increased incoming rocket fire early in the morning and that our landing would be a little unusual. It was the first time on the flight that I remember starting to get scared. About that time all of us noticed a Marine Corps F-4 fighter jet outside the window. There were actually two of them, one on each side.

I can't tell you how cool that looked and how afraid I was becoming. Like everyone else I hid it as best I could, but a silence fell over the cabin.

The captain came back on the intercom and told us to fasten our seat belts for our final approach to DaNang and that the Marine jets would escort us in. The flight attendants strapped in and signaled the cockpit, and almost immediately the plane took a steep dive downward. I could feel the G-force, and I kept watching the Marine F-4 follow us down right off our wingtip.

After what seemed a long time, the jet leveled off above the South China Sea, and just as the F-4 peeled off, I saw the tops of palm trees right below us on China Beach. Within seconds the plane was on the ground. There was very little taxi time, and the flight attendants got up and told us we would de-plane as quickly as possible.

As soon as the plane stopped, a mobile stairway was quickly positioned at the forward door, and the crew got us on our feet and out the door. They wished us good luck, each girl giving hugs and quick kisses to each Marine as he left the plane. These girls seemed so calm and brave while we were all nervous and scared. The Boeing 320 had a rear ramp door, and as we left out the forward door, Marines rotating back home were boarding via the rear ramp. In no time at all the plane was taxiing away and we were left on the hot tarmac feeling the first of many hot Vietnam days to come.

MY FIRST WEEK

After leaving the plane my memories become blurred, maybe because of the newness of being in Vietnam and just the awe of taking it all in. I seem to remember a large covered area, like a big green carport, covered, but open on the sides, and there were hundreds of sea bags stacked in a pile. At some point I was reunited with my sea bag although the memory is hazy. I must have been called by name and moved to a truck with other artillery Marine replacements. We were told we would be going to the 11th Marine Artillery Regiment.

I remember the smell of jet fuel, and it being very hot, and noisy, very noisy. Jets weren't the only aircraft coming and going. It was my first experience hearing the "thump, thump, thump" of military helicopters, a sound that still initiates a flood of memories to this day. Choppers were everywhere: Hueys, Sea Knights, Jolly Green Giants. It was very busy.

About an hour after we left the Continental jet, my fellow replacements and I left the airport, via truck, taking a short fifteen-minute drive to 11th Marine Headquarters. The headquarters compound was still inside DaNang but very close to two high hills on the western edge of the city. We checked in at the office and, after confirming orders, were sent to the supply hut for blankets, sheets, and a pillow. We asked about weapons and were told we would be issued M-16s at our final destination the next day. We wanted to be armed because we had already heard the rumors of large-scale attacks by the NVA (North Vietnamese Army) not only in DaNang but many other places as well. We also heard rumors that we would be sent north to a place called Khe Sahn, where a major battle was developing.

We left the supply hut and picked out cots in the transient tent. I remember seeing fear on the faces of the headquarters Marines, and it was obvious that they had not seen this level of combat activity before. It was also obvious that the HQ office Marines were glad they were staying in DaNang and we replacements were the ones leaving.

We finally stowed our gear, made up our cots, and then headed for the mess hall. The food actually looked pretty good. The main dish was some sort of chicken chow mien, and we all ate heartily because we weren't sure what the food would be like at our final destination. It soon became apparent that the meal was a problem, at least for me. At least one other replacement and I became violently ill.

It started about three hours after dinner when the regiment was called out on 100% alert with attacks eminent. We replacements, having no weapons, were sent to a small underground bunker and told to stay there. The bunker was about the size of a small bedroom with nothing but a dirt floor. Sitting on the dirt floor about 9 pm I knew something wasn't right, and soon I was running outside to throw-up along side my fellow replacement.

That was bad enough, but immediately the urge for a bowel movement was undeniable. There was a four-place outhouse a short distance away from the bunker, and I was soon so sick that I was sitting on the shitter seat for many minutes at a time. The diarrhea was extremely runny, and between my sick friend and me, we soon used up the two rolls of toilet paper that were available. We returned to the bunker asking the HQ Marines in the foxholes outside where we could get more toilet paper, but they only laughed and said none would be available until morning.

By this time I stank, and my friend and I were not allowed back in the bunker. That was only a momentary disappointment because I was soon back on the shitter with dripping diarrhea and no paper. I stayed there, not sure of what else I could do. Then the rocket attack started at DaNang Air Base a few miles away.

I had to do something, so I took off my skivvies and folded them as small as I could and wiped my rear. I ran back to the bunker and sat down as low as I could get alongside the sand bags rimming the outside of the bunker and watched the rockets hit near and far. I sat there sick, smelly, desperate with fear, and not really caring if an NVA rocket landed on me or not.

After a couple of hours and many return trips to the outhouse, my skivvies were saturated with feces. After the most miserable night of my life, the sun came up and I was able to find an outside wash area with faucets. I washed my underwear and dropped my pants to wash myself as best I could before returning to the transient hut to change clothes and collapse on my cot. The throwing up and the diarrhea were finished, but I was exhausted and slept through the day. I remember the HQ staff NCO coming through the tent looking for me, and when it was obvious I was sick, he left me saying that I would not be assigned until I was feeling better.

That night was much the same as the first, with occasional dry heaves, but no diarrhea. The rockets that started early in the morning continued throughout the night, and since I had slept all day, I watched the rockets and red tracers until dawn. I still could not bring myself to eat so I just had some apple juice. I spent the morning re-washing my soiled clothes and hanging them to dry. At lunch there was some soup and I tried a little. I felt a little nauseous and slept through dinner.

Later that night I started feeling much better and slept well except during the small arms and rocket fire. When the sun rose I realized that it was February 3rd, my 21st birthday. I remember thinking, "What a birthday present." I felt well enough to drink juice and eat toast for breakfast. It stayed down, and I was told to get my gear ready to move out.

While I was sick, other replacements were coming and going. Some got sick like me. I found myself with a new group of guys on a truck headed to a helicopter-landing zone (LZ) in DaNang. When we arrived, we placed our sea bags along a berm of dirt at the edge of the LZ and waited. There were hundreds of replacements, mostly grunts (infantry men), and as their names were called they boarded Sea Knights and headed north; only north, to the DMZ or Khe Sahn. The rumors were flying now as the returning helicopter crews were telling stories of major engagements and heavy enemy fire up north. I resigned myself to going north on a Sea Knight. I sat there the rest of the afternoon and finally my name was called for the next chopper. However, it was getting late and the next chopper never came. Those of us that were left got back on a truck in the fading light and returned to 11th Marine headquarters.

That whole night I thought about going north. I was able to eat again, but not very much. We were told to be ready early, and we knew we would be first to go when we reached the LZ in the morning.

It was a fitful sleep that night. I was worried about how I would act in combat. I was afraid but thankful I would be in a FDC (Fire Direction Control) bunker instead of being out on the guns in the open. Fear gripped me, and I didn't like it. Why did I have to go north?

As I thought of tomorrow's fate, my eventual destination, some three months in the future,

Thuong Duc Special Forces Camp, twenty-five miles southwest of DaNang, was being over-run that very night by a thousand NVA. So much for my twenty-first birthday.

It was dark when we awoke and sent to a hasty breakfast. Afterward we got our gear and stood in formation outside the HQ office. My name was called first, along with a few other FDC guys. The NCO said there was a change in orders and we four could return to our tent and wait for a truck to take us to 3rd Battalion. The rest of the replacements left for the LZ. Where was 3rd Battalion? No one had mentioned it in the rumors of the past few days.

We sat for an hour in the tent with our sea bags, and finally a deuce and a half truck pulled up with four of the saltiest looking Marines with flak jackets and M-16's. This truck and these Marines were not the DaNang Marines I had been looking at for the last four days. The truck had a heavy coating of red dirt and to a lesser extent, so did the Marines. The trucks and Marines in DaNang were relatively clean. I thought, "We're going way out somewhere; somewhere north."

A salty corporal took the orders from the HQ NCO, and after the brief roll call, told us to get on the truck. Within minutes we were on our way south! I have to admit that I was relieved to be going south after four days of rumors about how rough it was in the north.

The truck proceeded slowly through DaNang, stopping frequently for traffic jams. There were jeeps and trucks of every shape and kind packing the narrow asphalt roads. Supplies and men were going every which way. I got my first glimpse of daily life in Vietnam: the people, their faces, their clothes, their language, their houses; all of it new. After fifteen minutes we came to a stop at a guard station with a red and white barrier pole down across the road. I noticed rows of barbed wire extending out from the guard station, and I noticed that the asphalt stopped beneath us. This was the end of DaNang. The end of the paved road.

The barrier rose and the truck in front of us took off at full speed and a cloud of dust. We pulled forward to the barrier as it was lowered. The guard was staggering the trucks leaving Da Nang so they would not make as big a target. The corporal, who had been standing behind the cab of the truck with the other two armed Marines, turned toward us and told us to get down in the bed of the truck and lie on our sea bags. Then he turned to the other two Marines and said, "Lock and load." He and the two armed Marines took their M-16s and reversed the magazines, snapping a round in each of their chambers. "Hold on," the corporal said to us and the barrier was raised.

The truck took off, dust flying and gears grinding, reaching high speed in very little time. I thought, "This is it. I'm going to die before I get a weapon."

I think the truck was going as fast as it could because we were hauling ass. I peeked over the steel sides of the truck from time to time to see the lay of the land. Mostly flat land with dry cornfields and wet rice paddies. Every so often a clump of banana palms and grass huts would fly by. Our Marine guards were constantly looking in all directions as they hunched over the back of the truck's cab. The corporal would turn from time to time telling us to stay low. "I don't want anyone getting shot before I hand you over," he kept saying. He scared us pretty good, and we all thought he was John Wayne.

Finally, after what seemed like an hour, but was only probably twenty minutes, we slowed down as we approached the eastern finger of a low broad hill in the middle of the wide coastal plain. The corporal and his two Marines removed their magazines and ejected the rounds in the three M-16 chambers.

We were at Hill 55, headquarters for 3rd Battalion, 11th Marine Artillery, and 7th Marine Infantry Regiment. It consisted of five-finger ridges with the highest point in the middle. A sixty-foot wooden and metal tower stood at the apex with the huge FDC bunker below it.

We drove through the open barbed wire gate past salty Marines, a tent store, church, mess hall, countless bunkers, and wood and canvas huts with metal roofs. We stopped in front of the 3rd Battalion HQ hut next to two large diesel generators, one of which was humming along. The hut had a half dozen office personnel and just as many manual typewriters.

"Everybody out," the corporal shouted. We grabbed our sea bags and jumped out of the truck. A PFC came out of the hut and took our orders from the driver, and then the truck turned around and drove back to the other side of the hill. The PFC had us pick up our gear, and after checking our names against the orders, we followed him down the north finger past huts and ditches and bunkers. We passed two huge eight-inch self-propelled tracked guns, and a wooden basketball court before stopping at a canvas and wood hut or hooch and went inside.

There were rows of cots on each side of the tent hooch backed up against a plywood bulkhead half way up the side. A canvas tent covered the top half of the side and the roof was corrugated metal. Some of the cots were occupied with gear and fancy cabinets made out of large 105 howitzer ammo boxes. Outside on the north side facing the rice paddies was a deep ditch traversing the side of the hill. Beyond the ditch a few feet was a long, six-foot high, wall of stacked 105 wooden ammo boxes filled with dirt, and supported with metal T-posts forming a protective wall from rockets and small arms fire. This wall would protect the hooch while Marines were inside sleeping.

The four of us picked out empty cots, and I was fortunate to grab one with existing cabinets. Not only were these cabinets functional for holding gear and clothes, but also it formed a private cubicle of sorts. All around us were off duty Marines in various activities from sleeping and washing clothes to cleaning rifles and just hanging out. There was a diesel-filled open-air shitter, and five-gallon water cans for each hooch for drinking and cleaning, plus clotheslines and lots of sand bags.

After four days in Vietnam it was finally time to get our weapons. We stowed our sea bags on our cots and followed the PFC about thirty-five yards to a corrugated metal supply hut a little further down the hill. Inside, all of us were issued two blankets, rubber air mattress, jungle utilities, jungle boots, M-16's, ammo, Kevlar flak jackets, packs, ponchos, poncho liner (my favorite thing), ammo belts, magazines, canteens, first aid kits, helmets, K-bar fighting knives, and everything else we needed for combat.

I finally felt safe, if not secure, in the knowledge that I was armed with an M-16 and ammo. It was sort of surreal. Everyone walked around that hill armed twenty-four hours a day, seven days a week, and that took some getting used to.

We put on our flak jackets and helmets and slung our M-16s over our shoulders, and after picking up all the other gear, our little group headed outside. I was first in line as we walked along the top of the ditch back up to our hooch. I immediately heard the roar of jets to the north. About two miles away across the rice paddies was a group of Marine F-4 fighter jets dropping napalm on an area of palm trees by a bend in the river. My mates and I paused to watch, eyes riveted to the scene. It was amazing to see those jets in action, and I was quick to appreciate the fact that the NVA had no air cover in the south.

Watching that had lasted about fifteen seconds when the PFC yelled from the supply hut door to get moving. I again started walking up the hill and within a few steps I noticed a puff of dirt just ahead and then another and another. Then I noticed three guys up the hill at our hooch cowering in the ditch behind the rocket wall and waving frantically at us. More puffs of dirt! I turned back to my companions and was about to ask what was going on when I felt and heard this "whoosh!" fly past my head. It sounded like a freight train. Then it dawned on me and my fellow replacements that we were being shot at from the tree line two miles away. We were nose down in the ditch in mili-seconds and stayed there until the all clear was given.

After putting away and organizing our gear in the FDC hooch, the other replacements and I were able to joke about what had just transpired. Getting shot at is no laughing matter, but since the veteran guys were joking about it, calling us dumb-shits and so forth, it was better to laugh with them. One of the veteran FDC men, a corporal named Charlie from California who had been in country for seven months, came and got the four of us and took us up the hill to the FDC bunker.

Charlie was soft spoken, with a great smile and some junior college on his resume like me. He didn't seem to fit the Vietnam image of salty Marines, and to me he seemed an unlikely person to be in the Marine Corps. Of course, I didn't seem like that person either. Charlie was kind to us new guys and didn't use his rank to boss us around. He made a sincere attempt to start us out correctly, to limit our mistakes and keep us alive.

The FDC bunker was at the top center of Hill 55, south of the red dirt road that divided the hill into north and south halves. The sixty-foot rocket tower was directly across the road on the north side. The FDC bunker was the nerve center of 3rd Battalion artillery. It was dug down fifteen feet under ground with a timber and 2x12 wood roof covered with sand bags and a raised corrugated metal false roof on short 4x4 posts three feet above that. The false metal roof was there to detonate a rocket or mortar prematurely, thereby keeping the explosion from penetrating deep into the bunker.

There were two wooden and dirt stairways that led down into the bunker, one on the west side and one on the east side. The opening at the bottom led to a solid timber wall, and you had to turn right and then back to the left to get in. As a result, a small switchback corridor was formed with a ten-foot kill zone. This way an enemy zapper could not run straight into the bunker, and there would be a chance to kill him and limit his explosion to the corridor, thus saving lives in the main bunker.

There were also a series of foxholes around the bunker and its entrances that were manned by off duty FDC personnel when the possibility of attack was suspected. These times were always at night, and during the months of February and March it was every other night into the holes.

Inside the bunker were four main areas. The first and most prominent area was the FDC chart table. The chart table was a huge affair, a sort of drafting table made of 2x4s and plywood, and big enough for two independent chart stations. Above the charts, on the center partition, were colored maps of the battery fire zones for each battery in the battalion. The charts themselves were blank white plastic-type paper with black line grids, a thousand meters, or "one click," square.

The next area, on the other side of the center partition, and open between the 2x4 supports, was the computer table. There was room for two independent computers.

These are not the kind of computers you think about today; these computers were people, live Marines with charts, math tables, and slide rules. Every fire mission was worked up by a human computer and a chart man and checked by a back-up, thus two charts and chart men and two computer men. That fail-safe of two kept mistakes to a minimum. Short rounds or fire on the wrong target was unacceptable.

The third area all along the west side of the bunker was a communications table that held up to six radio operators at a time to communicate with the individual Artillery batteries and units of the 7th Marine Infantry Regiment that we supported. The radios that they used were battery operated PRC 25 (Portable Radio Communication), or "prick 25s" and were the same radios carried on the backs of operators in the field. Behind the radio table, against the wall, were boxes of olive drab colored D cell batteries and the operators would change the batteries quite frequently. So many batteries, so much expense in those alone.

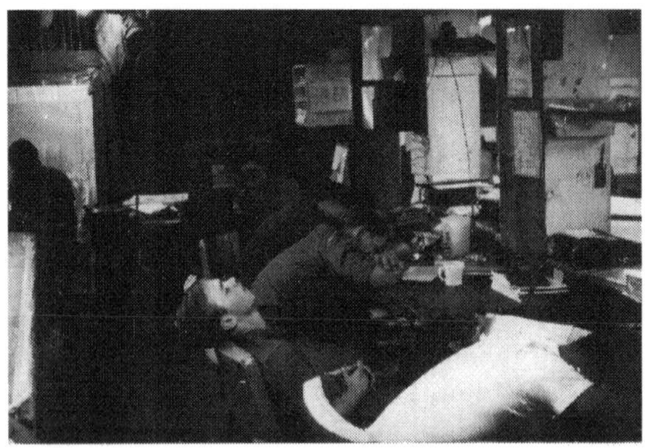

The last area was the south wall where the duty officer and the Naval Gunfire liaison officer had their desks. Usually these would be lieutenants or ensigns as in the case of the Naval Gunfire officer. The officers for the most part were good guys, and I was able to have a good relationship with one, Lt. C from Indiana.

During that first week we new guys spent a lot of time on the charts doing practice fire missions. We were all doing four hours on and four hours off shifts, and it was difficult sleeping as every twenty-four hours the sleep time changed by four hours. One day you had the twelve midnight to four in the morning shift, and the next you had the four in the morning to eight in the morning shift and so on. As I said before, there were two independent chart stations, and we took turns being the primary chart operator. We also did time as human computer although a corporal or lance corporal usually performed this job.

I became very proficient at being the computer, and the officers noticed my work. I made them aware of my age and college experience knowing that prepared me better than my nineteen-year-old co-replacements. This would become more important later as the Tet Offensive continued and we lost veteran FDC personnel to the outlying batteries, due to death, wounds, or regular rotations home.

Also during that week we had frequent real fire missions involving the two batteries on Hill 55 with us. Whiskey battery was a four-deuce mortar battery consisting of four large mortars. Whiskey Tango battery was a 155mm howitzer battery with four guns. There was also a self-propelled eight-inch battery of two guns, but their call sign slips my memory. The new guys, including myself, were on the charts backed up by veteran FDC guys.

Towards the end of that first week, early in the morning, a fire mission came in while the corporal doing computer duty was outside for a head call. Lt. C put me at the computers' station and he personally became my check computer. The fire mission came in for Whiskey battery and I was nervous, but was able to get through it quickly with no mistakes and had rounds on target in less then four minutes. Lt. C was happy with me and told me I would move up to the computer table during the slow daytime shifts. I was pleased and relieved that I had performed well in my first real test. Lt. C said all of us new privates would be promoted to PFC at the end of the month if we continued to do well.

After a few jokes about being teacher's pet from the other guys, I finished my shift at four in the morning and went to sleep eager to return at eight for my daylight shift. It would not be what I expected. After a quick breakfast I reported for duty at the FDC bunker as usual. Seems as though FDC had to supply a warm body for mess duty every day, and the men took turns for the two-week intervals.

Since I was one of the newest replacements and never had mess duty in boot camp or ITR, I was picked. That really upset me. Not only was I not going to move into the computer chair, but also I heard that no one got promoted from mess duty. My two weeks of mess duty would take me into March 2nd, and promotions were only as of the first of any month. I picked up my M-16, flak jacket, and helmet, and walked back to the mess hall to report for mess duty.

MESS HALL DUTY WITH THE FOUR SEASONS

I reported to the mess sergeant and, after stowing my helmet, flak jacket, and locking my rifle in a spare room, I donned a white paper hat and wore just my white t-shirt, utility pants and boots for mess duty.

I reported to a corporal who looked very familiar. I soon came to realize that it was the same salty corporal that scared the death out of me on the ride to Hill 55. He wasn't John Wayne after all, but instead he was a cook. He laughed when I reminded him of the trip.

"You guys were pretty scared hugging your sea bags on the truck bed," he said.

I could see the humor in it now, but not then.

I was put in charge of the two milk dispensing machines and the five gallon ice cream containers and just had to keep the milk and ice cream supplied at all times. I had to wipe the spills, too. When morning mess was over I was one of many guys setting out to clean the tables, counters, and floors. The mess hall doors closed, and as I started to clean my first table, the loud speaker inside the mess hall blared out, "Sheeeeery, Sherry baby, Sher..eer..ry." It was the greatest hits album of Frankie Valli and the Four Seasons. Seems as though the mess sergeant had an old turntable and one album. For three hours we heard "Sherry", "Big Girls Don't Cry", "Dawn Go Away", "Ronnie", "Rag Doll" and the rest, over and over again. And just to piss off the NVA, he played it as loud as it would go.

By the second day I was singing along with Frankie like everyone else, and by the end of the third day I knew every song and every lyric by heart.

The duty wasn't so bad. We worked from 6:00 a.m. to 9:00 p.m. and got eight hours of sleep except when we were on 100% alert, and then I had to man one of the foxholes around the FDC bunker all night. On those days the mess sergeant gave us a half hour here and there to take catnaps as best we could. Every day except Sunday there were three meals a day; only breakfast and dinner on Sunday.

On my second Sunday I was deemed a veteran of the Vietnam mess hall and as such I was included in a group of cooks and other mess duty short-timers that took the twenty-minute trip into DaNang to spend the day at China Beach. This ride was more enjoyable then the first.

I could not believe this place. It was like being back in the states only with no girls. There were hamburger and hot dog stands, Cokes and beer everywhere. You had to pay for it though, and the beach was awesome. There must have been a thousand guys on the beach, most of them from right in DaNang, but some real combat companies as well. I didn't consider myself a combatant, although I was one step closer than the DaNang Marines. After three weeks on Hill 55, I was fairly sure that any enemy attack would be repelled quickly. Mortars and rockets would be the only demons to face as our firepower would be quite substantial.

The beach was like any beach in California with nice big waves and a dangerous undertow.

They cautioned us not to go in above the waist. Oh, and there was one other thing: SHARKS. Every twenty seconds a Huey helicopter would speed by at wave top level. Back and forth they flew all afternoon. I was told it was to keep the sharks away, but I'm not sure that was true. More than likely the pilots were just showing off.

I must have eaten three hot dogs and three hamburgers each in two hours with lots of cold Coke. I was never much of a beer drinker, but some of the guys on the beach got pretty drunk. I would imagine they were combat troops not in a position to get beer very often. After a couple of hours we headed back to Hill 55 to get ready for dinner.

One of my last days in the main mess hall provided a glimpse of war I had not experienced before. As I mentioned before, there was a lot of artillery and administration staff on the hill, but there was always a large contingent of 7th Marines coming out of the field for two or three weeks at a time. Their main task at Hill 55 was perimeter security, and they sent out a squad to patrol the perimeter of the hill each day.

One afternoon at lunch we heard small arms fire off the southeast finger of the hill, and a lot of the guys got up from lunch and looked out the south windows. I was manning the milk machines again when a Marine ran into the mess hall and yelled that the perimeter squad from 2/7 was engaged with an unknown NVA force. Half the mess hall emptied within seconds. Guys were running down the southeast finger putting on their helmets and flak jackets and loading magazines into their M-16's. Those were *their* 7th Marines out there, and all those guys were running down the hill into that small arms fire. At first I thought they were crazy, but then I realized how brave they were to do that without orders. I was never so proud to be a Marine as I was at that point. I just hoped I could react the same some day.

My last two days of mess duty were spent in the officers' mess. I had graduated to waiter and busboy for the officers. I saw all of my officers from the bunker including Lt. C, and I hoped we would find time to talk, but I soon realized that it wouldn't happen here. He was not the same in front of the other officers. Of course he couldn't be. Our eyes met as he left and he said, "Cowart, how many days you have left on mess?"

I answered, "Two." That was all we said. I wanted to ask him if I could still get promoted with the others, but it wasn't my place.

We had a visitor on the Hill the next day, and I was in position to serve Captain Robb his breakfast that morning. For those that don't know, Captain Robb was a bit of a celebrity in the Marine Corps. He was married to President Lyndon Johnson's daughter, and Johnson was still President at that time. You had to give him credit. He didn't use his clout to get out of going to Vietnam.

The next morning the FDC had formation, and promotions were the main attraction. I was heart broken. I was cleaning a table and feeling sorry for myself when everyone else got their stripes.

BACK TO THE FDC

On March 3rd, 1968 I reported back to the FDC. It was eight in the morning, and they wanted me to work a full eight hours and then start my four on and four off at 4:00 p.m. I worked the charts all morning specifically to get me into war ready shape again. There were new guys I had not worked with before, and they struggled with the charts. I had not lost my touch and was sitting at the back watching the others practice when Sgt. L came in just before noon and handed me two black PFC collar badges.

"Put these on," he said. "You were promoted on the first."

I couldn't believe it. I thought I was left behind again. I was very happy. A short time later Lt. C came into the bunker. He came over and asked if I was ready for the computer table again, and I said sure. He turned to Sgt. L and told him to make me practice the rest of the afternoon and that when I started the eight to midnight shift, I would be in the computer chair.

New PFC stripes on my collars and being at the computer table again; boy, I was beaming! I practiced that afternoon, went to evening chow, where I knew all the cooks by name, and traded pleasant insults with them as I passed down the chow line. After trying to sleep a little, I returned to the FDC bunker for the eight to midnight shift, and since it was a quiet evening, I sat at the computer table talking with Lt. C most of the shift. The war aside, life felt good again, even if only for the evening.

THE ROCKET TOWER

As the FDC brass gained trust in me and the other new men, a few of us were picked to do duty on the rocket tower. The rocket tower was a sixty-foot high structure made out of 4x6 beams. At the top was a ten-foot square platform surrounded by a four-inch thick wooden wall. Behind the wall on all sides was a layer of stacked sand bags. A roof of wooden beams, corrugated metal and sand bags finished the upper structure. In order to get up to the top level, one had to climb a wooden ladder enclosed with corrugated metal sewer pipe cut in half and secured to the wood structure. The metal pipe was fixed from the eight-foot level all the way to the top. Not only did it protect against bullets and shrapnel, but also it protected one from slipping and falling off the ladder.

At the top, the tools of war included a PRC 25 radio, a battery commander's scope, chart table and charts, night vision binoculars, and an instrument for shooting an azimuth to target. The basic job description entailed searching the surrounding countryside for rocket launching sites, and when observing one, shooting a direction azimuth to the target and calling battalion right away with the reading. The whole valley and coastal plain was dotted with outposts and rocket towers, and the idea was to get a triangulation on a rocket site with at least two other rocket towers. If this was done properly, artillery rounds could be on target within a few minutes in hopes of catching the enemy still there. Of course, it was not an exact science, but even if we were just close, twelve rounds of howitzer fire nearby must have scared the shit out of them. It goes without saying that most of these missions were at night.

The other job description was that of forward observer. The battery commander's scope was a periscopic binocular on a tripod that allowed one to search the tree lines around Hill 55 while staying below the sandbag layer on the tower. It was used mostly during the day. Most of the time nothing happened, but on occasion a perimeter patrol would get into trouble and would ask for artillery support. One such incident happened to me.

My first four-hour shifts were during the daylight hours when little or nothing happened. We had practiced radio procedures the previous weeks, and I got very comfortable on the radio. One day in late March I was in the tower between the noon and four shift when a fire mission from 7th Marines came in. It was from a jungle/swamp area about a mile away to the south. The Marine on the radio called in a grid and azimuth to target and asked for an adjusting round of white phosphorus. He said they were taking heavy machine gun fire from some hooches to the west. I could hear the gunfire now and swung the battery commander's scope around to the south. I soon found the tracer fire and knew our guys were to the east firing west. I scoped the hooches and when the WP round hit, I let battalion know my azimuth to target. From my azimuth, I told the FDC to adjust fire left 200 meters. The ground Marine called for a left 100 adjust, drop 100 from his azimuth, which would have been add 100 from my azimuth. The FDC worked up both our data and fired another WP round. I was watching when it hit only meters from the first hooch. I called in round on target, but the ground Marine asked for another left 50 and fire for effect. Within a minute 8 rounds of 155mm howitzer fire landed around and on the hooches. The small arms fire lessened and the ground Marine called for helicopter gunship support and medivac.

I continued to watch as the Marines engaged in sporadic fire. When the first Huey showed up, I watched through the battery commander's scope as the M-60 machine gunners poured in fire at the enemy position. Next a Sea Knight showed up and started an approach to pick up the wounded, and as they neared the ground, the enemy machine gun started again. I watched as the Sea Knight took hits. The 50 cal. machine gunners on the Sea Knight were blasting everything in front of them. I watched as palm trees and hooches were cut in half by the intense fire. Dust everywhere and finally the Sea Knight's rotors stopped as they hit the ground. I confirmed with the FDC that a Sea Knight was down and that enemy fire had continued. More helicopters entered the battle, and shortly the only fire was from our guys. Finally another Sea Knight landed under cover fire and removed the downed crew and the wounded grunts. I continued to watch and monitor the radio for Battalion.

Soon my shift was over and all the fire had subsided. I would miss seeing the removal of the downed Sea Knight, but all in all it was an exciting scene to watch and be involved in. I would tell the story over and over again at my next FDC shift because the guys in the bunker, who could only listen on the radio, wanted to hear my eyewitness report.

The rest of March found us with many rocket target fire missions and nights of 100% alert. The only other unique experience on the tower happened on one of my last nights. At night and some days we usually had a 7th Marine grunt come up with us as sort of a backup in case we needed someone to shoot enemy sappers trying to place explosives at the base of the tower or shoot any enemy trying to climb the ladder. That way we could continue to do our job without having to defend the position.

One night I had this crazy eighteen-year-old with me who must have seen too much combat. He kept asking me if I had any souvenirs. I said no, that this tower and the bunker were all I had ever done. Then he told me about how he had these NVA ears and how he would sell me one. I told him no thanks. He took offense and asked why I didn't want one; was I a gook lover or something? I did not want to be on this crazy guy's bad side so I thought quickly and told him I wanted to cut off an ear on my own. I wanted to be in combat like him. That raised my stock in his eyes, and I just listened to his crazy talk until the shift was up. He asked me to let him know if any other rear-area MF's would like to buy one, and I said I would. Luckily I never saw him again.

Standing 100% alert those first weeks were a combination of unquestioned fear and anticipation. Part of me wanted no part of any NVA attack and part of me was tired of the all-nighters and wished they would attack and walk into our firepower. The NVA must have known it would be suicide to attack Hill 55, because our firepower would have been awesome. I would sit in that red dirt hole, staring down the hill in the black darkness waiting for tracers from the front line Marines. I would wonder what it would be like to kill someone up close, or if I would hesitate firing my weapon. I thought not, but I had heard stories of just that.

The NVA never did do anything on the ground except probing the wire with a couple of AK-47 bursts that lasted a few seconds.

Rockets and mortars were a different story. During March and April we took quite a few rockets, and their reliability was not very good. Most were 122mm Chinese-made rockets that had terrible accuracy, and many did not explode, instead breaking in half and spilling out their contents of powder, nails, bits of metal, broken glass, and other items intended to cause wounds. The sound of the rocket in flight was not pleasant.

Mortars I hated, and luckily there were few incoming mortars in those months. I hated the sound of mortars more then anything. It was terrifying after a while, and I quickly understood why Marines under constant barrage, like those at Khe Sahn, would develop shell shock.

FREE TIME ON THE HILL

When not on duty, most of the time was spent eating or sleeping. On occasion we would be digging new foxholes or repairing old ones around the FDC bunker. Filling sand bags with the red dirt of the hill was never a fun job. The coarse red dirt would mix with your sweat making for a scratchy situation. The ground itself was very rocky and hard, requiring picks and thick metal bars to break it.

However, there were lighter times. It amazes me now how many good times we had. Any civilian being asked to spend a day in Vietnam on Hill 55 would be scared beyond belief, but one gets used to the boredom that war is most of the time, and to keep our sanity we had to joke around.

During my first week on Hill 55, a new replacement named Norris arrived on the hill. He was the tallest Marine I had ever seen. I'm six feet four inches tall, and he towered over me. He had a great sense of humor and was always in the middle of a good time.

Since I had a camera, a lot of posing in front of it was good sport. Norris, the other FDC guys, and I staged some goofy pictures to send home, giving our loved ones a sense of safety and well being. I also took pictures of my gear, M-16, and everyday shots of all the weapons around me. I wanted proof that I was here in this situation, and I wanted to remember it and show it to any children, family, and friends I might have in the future. I didn't think I would ever write a book, but the pictures are now helping give the reader of this book a sense of being there, too.

Along with the other chores of cleaning one's self and one's gear, there was the joy of beer drinking. Most of the guys liked beer, but I didn't. They had to buy it for 25 cents a can, and although most of the guys sent their pay home as I did, we all kept a little in the form of Vietnam Piastors: colorful bills printed by the US military for use in buying goods in-country. I spent my money on 35mm slide film and processing, and the occasional Coke.

I also purchased an old reel-to-reel Sony tape recorder and wrote a letter to the local Seattle rock and roll radio station, and they sent me back a tape of songs. I would play it over and over again, and the guys liked it. We couldn't get good reception from Armed Forces Radio in DaNang at that time, so my tape was put to good use.

The most important free time was mail time. As any one who was ever in the military, especially combat, will tell you, mail was the most important thing to a service man or woman. Getting mail was what kept us going, with the realization that we had 290 days and a wake-up to go.

Mail from girlfriends and girls in particular were the best. And pictures; pictures of girls to show your buddies were priceless. The occasional package from Mom contained goodies that were never hoarded, but passed around.

I remember getting a letter from my mom and noting that it was written on a Sunday morning. My thoughts turned to Sunday morning back home and how easy Sunday mornings were: lounging around reading the Sunday funnies and waiting for the weekly NFL game to come on TV. I remember thinking of peanut butter and raspberry jam sandwiches with a cold glass of milk chaser, of washing my car, or throwing the football around with friends.

One time my mom sent a package with a new food item I had never seen before. Individual little servings of chocolate pudding with pull-off tops. They tasted so good, but there were only six, and I only got two of them before the guys around me attacked. Simple things and activities from home became huge memories in the red dirt of Vietnam.

SURVEY OP

On April 1st, 1968, the off duty FDC personnel had an informal formation, and to my surprise I received a combat meritorious promotion to Lance Corporal, E-3. I had been a private, E-1, from 7 Aug 1967 in boot camp until 28 February 1968; seven months. I was a PFC, E-2, for one month. I was stunned to say the least, but very proud. With the promotion came new duties, and one of the first was leaving Hill 55 on a survey mission with Sgt. L. It was my first time on a Sea Knight helicopter, and I can hardly put into words how excited I was to see that rear door ramp open, hear the beat of those rotors close up, and run into that chopper like a real combat veteran. Did I mention that I was also scared to death?

Sgt. L had picked me to go the day before. Most Marines didn't know that one of FDC's job descriptions was gun emplacement survey. We only covered it in artillery school for a couple of days so all of the replacements, myself included, had pretty much forgotten the routine, but Sgt. L was the HQ battalion survey expert, and I was going to become proficient enough to replace him when he rotated home. At least that was what he said at the time. I remember our survey instrument was called a Theodolite-16, or T-16 for short. Sgt. L carried the T-16 and tri-pod, and I carried the tall red and white stakes.

We boarded the chopper that usually carries sixteen Marines in full battle gear, but he and I were the only passengers. I followed Sgt. L's lead and ran into the back of the chopper and sat down next to him on a fold down canvas and aluminum bench seat. Almost simultaneously, both the 50-caliber machine gunner and Sgt. L motioned for me to move to the opposite side of the Sea Knight. Just like in a boat, it's best to distribute the weight. My adrenalin must have been soaring as the Sea Knight shook into flight. I was so excited and so scared. Hill 55 had become a place of relative safety over the last two months, and I was heading south into the area around Tam Ky that they called the Arizona Bad Lands because of the many daily firefights with the NVA.

I had my helmet, flak jacket, M-16, ten loaded magazines (180 rounds), an extra bandoleer of ammo (another 180 rounds), a small pack with poncho, poncho liner, C-rations, full canteen, first aid kit, two M-26 grenades, and E-tool. While on tower duty with the occasional 7th Marine, I had heard stories of the guys running out of ammo so instead of the usual 180 rounds, I doubled up. I knew the extra weight was no problem because I was flying, not humping.

After a fairly short ten-minute flight, we circled a red dirt blotch on the green landscape where they dug out an LZ and drifted slowly down for a landing. There were lots of Marines filling sand bags and making foxholes, ditches, and bunkers. There was some heavy equipment, a dozer and a smaller backhoe helping shape things up. The engineers had already built a rocket tower and placed timbers for large bunkers. There were a few large tents including a mess tent so we weren't going to need the C-rations.

The gun battery wasn't on site yet, and Sgt. L found the liaison officer who told us where to survey in the gun positions. He suggested we pick out a place to sleep for the night, so we found some room in a ditch well inside the wire next to some grunts and set up our ponchos as a tent. We placed some sand bags around us for a defensive position and started in the survey work.

The work was boring, and as the day closed, we knocked off surveying and headed for the mess tent. It was good we did, because as soon as we were finished eating and taking a head call, darkness was setting in. There was no electricity at this outpost, only a few kerosene lanterns, and those were at the HQ tent and obscured from vision. It got really dark. We couldn't see two feet in front of us, and the only time we left our hole was to piss a few feet away. It was pretty scary for me, but Sgt. L slept like a baby. My sleep was fitful and this wasn't even the real bush.

The night passed calmly with very little distant small arms fire once or twice in the night. Our perimeter was not tested, and the next day we got to work early. We finished that afternoon, and Sgt. L radioed we were through, but there were no Sea Knights available to pick us up until morning.

I took this as a bad omen as I was anxious to get home to the relative safety of Hill 55. As it turned out, the night once again passed without incident and even though I was dreaming up all kinds of survival battle scenarios, it was not to be. The flight back to Hill 55 the next morning was pleasant, and when we landed and ran off the chopper with our special survey gear, there were some new guys, clean and shiny, with stateside utilities, standing nearby and watching us, eyes glued, as we departed the Sea Knight. Making eye contact, I knew how they felt. They thought I was a bad ass with my dirty clothes and my M-26s hanging from my belt. I stood a little taller. I enjoyed them thinking I was a real combat vet.

MAMELUKE THRUST

I settled back into the routine of four on, four off, FDC, and rocket tower, and I finally started to think I would survive this war. A lot of the guys I had come in with were gone to the outer batteries, Golf, Hotel, and India. They kept me at HQ because I was older and I was good. I became a watch sergeant even though I was a lance corporal, and I took charge of the fire missions on my watch. I trained the new guys and became very comfortable in my situation.

However there was one guy I just couldn't get through to. He was a Mexican-American lance corporal named Jesus. We called him Jesse, and I'm not sure he like that. I felt he had a chip on his shoulder and needed to prove he was better than any one else. I think he was upset that I made lance corporal so quickly as it had taken him longer. He was good; very good. He was no dummy. I wanted to be his friend and so did the others, but he was cold and distant. We figured he didn't like white people. We had no other Hispanics in the FDC; a few on the guns, along with a few blacks, but the FDC was a white man's world for all practical purposes, fair or not.

Toward the last week of April a new operation called Mameluke Thrust was beginning to take shape, and Golf battery was going mobile to support the 7th Marines whose job it was to take back a hill to the west called Thuong Duc. It was almost off our maps. It had been overrun my third day in Vietnam and still had not been re-secured.

It was a camp for Green Beret Special Forces, and a new twelve man A-Team with their South Vietnamese Rangers were eager to re-establish their position. The 7th Marines were picked to fight their way back up the Thuong Duc Valley and support the Green Berets. Golf 3/11 was going to support both units with their six 105 howitzers.

I had heard the name Thuong Duc before and knew it was a bad place. No one wanted to go there. Cpl. C and some of the older vets had been reassigned to Golf battery because they needed veterans for this dangerous operation. By the second week in May 1968 Operation Mameluke Thrust had been underway for a week, and we monitored the action on our radios. Only India battery was far enough out to reach them for additional support, but they would be moving further west into the Thuong Duc Valley and surrounding mountains shortly.

One afternoon I had the rocket tower shift. My radio was not on the frequency they used for Mameluke Thrust; only the FDC radiomen could call them, and only inside the FDC bunker could you hear the goings on. The Operation had been stalled, and Golf battery was on a large sand bar on the north side of the Song Vu Gia River that flowed out of the Thuong Duc Valley. This much I had known from the night before.

Golf battery was taking daily and nightly incoming mortar fire and small arms fire. At about 3:30 in the afternoon, up in the tower, on or about the 15th of May 1968, I got a call on the radio from the FDC bunker below me. They said they were sending a man up early to relieve me and that I was to report to the bunker ASAP.

They no sooner signed off before I noticed one of the guys I trained on his way up. I don't remember exactly who it was, but the Marine told me that something awful was happening in the

Thuong Duc Valley on that sand bar. I grabbed my rifle and descended the caged ladder in record time. When I got to the bunker, Lt. C told me I had been picked as a replacement with two other men from FDC and to get to the LZ in full battle gear. I remember Jesse being on watch, and after hearing the Lt., he volunteered. In that split second, I first didn't want him along because he hated everyone, but then I realized he needed this to prove himself. I knew he was the best one besides me. I, however, didn't need to prove anything, and would have rather stayed on Hill 55.

The other guy, if I remember correctly, was Norris, and the three of us ran out of the bunker and down the hill to gear up. Sgt. L found us getting ready in our hooch and gave us suggestions on what to take. He didn't want me to take my camera, but I insisted. If I was going into battle I wanted proof. I still didn't know the specifics, only that some Marines in the FDC had been killed.

Sgt. L went with us to the LZ and waited with us for the Sea Knight. Some other Marines joined us; gun grunts I supposed, and soon we saw and heard the chopper heading our way. Sgt. L was so serious; I knew this was no survey mission. I could see the concern in his eyes. I was so scared, but I was in charge of our little group for the moment, and I couldn't let Jesse or Norris see my fear. They probably did anyway. I know they were scared too, and Jesse would soon wish he never volunteered. I said goodbye to Sgt. L and boarded the Sea Knight. It was my third trip in a chopper.

That afternoon on that sand bar in the Thuong Duc Valley an enemy mortar had hit a million to one shot. Golf battery's FDC was in a mobile amtrack, an amphibious tracked vehicle, similar to a big box with a forward opening ramp door for coming and going. The ramp was open and was protected by a six-foot high sand berm. The position, as I have said earlier, was being mortared day and night at various times. The first mortar fired that afternoon hit the open ramp of the amtrack at such an angle as to spray the inside full of hot shrapnel. The FDC lieutenant, watch sergeant, and one FDC chart man were killed and three more FDC men wounded.

The ensuing battle left more wounded, and as we neared the sand bar LZ, the crew chief yelled at us to get off quick. We were landing in a hot LZ. It was taking mortar and small arms fire, and there were wounded waiting to get back on.

I had never landed in a hot LZ, and Jesse, Norris and the others, as far as I knew, had never been in a Sea Knight, let alone flying into live fire. I could not hide my fear now, and as I looked at the others no one said a word. We were all were scared to death. We were close now, and the sounds of explosions rose above the sound of the rotors. The rear ramp was opening while still in flight, and when we landed with a thump, we were on our feet running out the back. There was smoke and noise and dirt and sand everywhere. Total chaos! Jesse and I ran side by side and landed face down in a sandy ditch as other Marines loaded a few wounded on our chopper. The mortars landed all around. Everyone ran for cover, and the Sea Knight lifted off and away unscathed. As far as I can remember, Jesse and I didn't move until the mortars stopped. I looked around not saying anything and saw the amtrack nearby. Cpl. C half walked, half crawled, out of it and we headed for him. Cpl. C told Jesse, Norris, and me the whole story as we huddled behind the sand berm. They were already referring to the amtrack as the *coffin* and it was the first time I didn't like being in FDC. The NVA knew the amtrack was the nerve center and would target it above all else.

We asked where to stow our gear, and Cpl. C said dig a hole, a deep one, and share it. So Jesse and I got to work digging a hole near the amtrack. Cpl. C also told us that this wasn't like Hill 55. Passwords meant something out here, and if you didn't know the password after dark, you better not move all night.

Just before dark we got mortared again, and although it only lasted a few minutes, it was horrifying. I hated mortars; I never got used to them. They kept Jesse and me together on the same watch, and after our four hours, we returned to our hole and tried to sleep. It wasn't cold, and we slept back-to-back trying not to touch each other. I had lost track of Norris and found out he had been returned to Hill 55. Someone said it was because he was too tall to fit in the amtrack.

The battery fired on and off all night. I had not seen so many fire missions before. There was small arms fire all around us, too, as the NVA tested the wire a few times each night. All the next day Sea Knights would supply us mostly with M-

16 ammo and 105mm rounds. Off duty men would be picked to off-load the stuff, and it was dangerous because the mortars started firing as soon as a Sea Knight got close.

That sand bar was a hellhole. Across the river were two tall jungle ridges where the NVA artillery was massed, and we targeted those ridges every time anyone saw a puff of smoke rise. In the flat valley on both sides of the river the 7th Marines and the NVA infantry were fighting it out whenever they made contact. There was no pretending now. Jesse and I were true combat veterans, and we did our job on that sand bar. We knew the guys back on Hill 55 and Hill 65 (India battery) were listening to our radio traffic and were thanking God they weren't with us. I was proud of myself and Jesse and the other FDC guys for performing under such unimaginable stress while all the time being scared shitless.

THE CHINAMAN

We spent another few days on that sand bar, and as the 7th Marines made their way west we would have to follow, right to Laos if need be. The last night we were on the sand bar an odd thing happened. As a rule both the NVA and Marines in no way wanted to leave their wounded and dead out on the battlefield for the other to see. When our wire was attacked nightly, we would return fire and kill and wound the enemy, but come daylight all that could be found were bloodstains and a few body parts. That last night was different. An enemy sapper had breached the wire and was killed before he could reach the amtrack and set off his satchel charge. Jesse and I were working the FDC shift inside the bunker when the attack took place. When our shift was over the lieutenant told us about the sapper and took us to him.

Yes, he was dead. He had a few bullet holes in his side and back, and he was naked from the waist up. The lieutenant told us he would have killed us that night if he had made it to the amtrack. The lieutenant then said, "What's wrong with this picture?" Jesse and I couldn't venture a guess. "Look at his face, arms and upper body." We looked again and realized that his face didn't look Vietnamese. He was sort of fat, or at least well fed, and he had a bulky upper body.

"He's Chinese, I'd bet my life on it. A red Chinese," the lieutenant said.

The Lieutenant was right. He didn't look like any skinny Vietnamese man or boy I had ever seen. We pulled the blanket back over him and returned to our hole. Jesse and I didn't talk much; he was still distant even though we shared a hole. He probably thought I was distant too. We didn't talk about this either. We just went to sleep.

WEST TO THUONG DUC

After five days we pulled up stakes and headed west. The awful ridge across the river was quiet now and we needed to follow the 7th Marines further west into the Thuong Duc Valley. We loaded the trucks at daybreak, and as we left the sand bar, the local Vietnamese swarmed into our vacated position.

They were scavenging anything of use they could get out of our temporary garbage dump. There wasn't much there, mostly old C-ration cans and broken wood from ammo boxes.

It was the first time in six days that we had not been taking incoming rounds on the sandbar, and as I packed up my gear I realized my camera had been in my pack the whole time. With the constant threat of mortars, day and night, I had forgotten about it. Now I took it out of the case and put it around my neck. I took a few pictures of the ridge and the sandbar as we were leaving. I also saw a LAW (Light Antitank Weapon) sitting inside the amtrack, so I took it and strapped it on with my M-16.

The convoy of trucks towing howitzers pulled out of the sand bar and moved slowly onto the dirt road heading west. All along the route were squads of 7th Marines providing security, and blending in with the foliage on the side of the road. Every so often, further up on the ridge, we would see more Marines making their way west. Sometimes one would wave, and we would wave back from our truck. I continued to take pictures as we drove west, and after an hour we were beginning to feel comfortable about the trip west. We had taken no enemy fire and all was quiet. That was about to change.

Our destination was an old French airstrip from the fifties situated just below the Special Forces Camp at Thuong Duc. I had just taken a picture of the truck and howitzer in front of us when mortar rounds started hitting a couple of hundred yards ahead. The convoy halted, and we took cover behind the truck bed walls. The mortars were coming from the ridge on the right and from the reverse slope. I could see 7th Marines working up the hill some distance ahead.

The road dipped down with a sharp left hand turn at the bottom of a gully where the trucks had to slow way down. Great spot for an ambush, and the NVA had already adjusted the spot. We started moving again, but kept lots of distance between trucks this time. We stopped again and could see the gully ahead. They were having one truck at a time race through the turn and up the other side while the Marines on the ridge shot covering fire back down the other side. A few mortars landed next to two trucks ahead, but the next two got through without incoming.

It was our turn now, and we headed down into the gully. When we reached the bottom, our truck driver tried to down shift to a lower gear for the run up the other side and killed the engine. There we were, sitting at the bottom when a mortar landed about twenty feet away. The six of us on the back knew they were trying to hit the truck so we hopped out and took cover. Two more mortars hit way off target, and a 7th Marine sergeant yelled out at us to get back in the truck or we'd be walking with them. The truck was moving now so we had to run and pull ourselves up. Two of the guys didn't make it and had to double-time up the hill on the other side. They finally caught up to us when we stopped. The driver was pretty new and very nervous, but he joked about it, and we all were glad things had worked out okay.

After our brush with the mortars, the convoy formed up and slowly headed into the Thuong Duc village area where the old French airstrip was. As we rolled past rice paddies, tree lined hooches, and kids; I snapped a picture showing Thoung Duc Special Forces Camp above and beyond the village. It was my first trip to Thuong Duc and I could imagine the NVA swarming down the ridge above the Special Forces Camp and over running it. I was glad we were staying in the valley at the airstrip.

The old French airstrip was centered in the field to the right of the dirt road as we approached the village. It was surrounded on three sides by rice paddies, and the fourth or roadside was a cornfield. The strip was about a thousand feet long and 100 feet wide, so our guns and trucks were spread out in a long narrow defensive position. The amtrack was in the center closer to the cornfield side, and this was where we FDC men would defend it. Back on the sand bar we were in the absolute middle of a circular perimeter, but now we were exposed in a long narrow rectangle perimeter. Before, when attacked, we never were at the wire and thus never had to fire our M-16s as

Marines were in front of us. This time we would be sleeping and fighting right at the wire, with our men stretched thin.

That first afternoon and night we barely had time to start stringing wire and digging holes and ditches before it started raining. Jesse and I dug a long shallow hole and filled sand bags with the dirt, and later, mud. We placed them around the top and cornfield side of the hole and in the bottom. The row of sand bags on the bottom of the hole kept us from sleeping in the mud. It was still awful, and even though it was 70 plus degrees at night, being wet was a cold affair. When Jesse and I finally tried to sleep, we laid down with our poncho liners back to back. After a while we were cold and wet enough to stop trying not to touch each other, and lay there touching backs to keep warm. It was a weird sensation, and Jesse and I never talked about it; we just did it when we were cold.

We were probed about 2:00 in the morning with AK-47 fire on the east end of the airstrip. The fire was coming from the cornfield side as expected, because crawling up on the rice paddy side would be awfully miserable, even for the Viet

Cong. Jesse and I woke up and grabbed our M-16s. We watched as the green and red tracers were flying into the east end of the airstrip and our guys were firing back red tracers into the cornfield. Pop flares were shot, and the resulting flare on a parachute lit up the sky around the airstrip. The firefight only lasted about two minutes, and then as the flare touched the wet ground, all was quiet again until one of the lieutenants came down the line. He was pissed.

He yelled at all of us FDC and gun grunts around the amtrack saying, "What the hell were you guys doing? We had a battle here, and I didn't see any fire coming from this end."

We all looked at each other and one guy said, "I didn't know I was supposed shoot down that way." He spoke for all of us because we had never been in a firefight before.

The lieutenant yelled, "Next time there is any fire on this side of the line along its entire length, and you have a clear shot at where the enemy tracers are coming from, I want to see LEAD FLYING out of these holes! You got that?"

"Yes, sir," we all said. He left swearing to himself, and we returned to our holes. We couldn't sleep when it was our turn, because it started raining again and because we were looking for another attack along the line before daybreak. It never came and the sun rose, greeted by about a hundred Marines who were wet, muddy and cold.

We spent the morning trying to dry our wet gear and cleaning our rifles and magazines. Tonight would be different, and we talked a little about that as we ate C-rations for breakfast. It was my time to man the FDC, and I entered the amtrack with the other three guys on duty. We had a new lieutenant, Lt. V, and he didn't say much to us or us to him. After an hour one of the guys came in and said that some of the 7th Marines were at the west end of the airstrip, and they were swimming and washing their clothes in a smaller tributary that joined the main river a couple hundred meters to the south. He asked the sergeant if our guys could do the same. The sergeant left to check it out and soon all the off duty guys were down at the river swimming and washing the mud off their utilities.

That day we had four 155mm self-propelled tracked howitzers join us on the airstrip along with a tank from 1st Tanks. We now were a pretty formidable battle group. As I sat on the amtrack ramp warming in the morning sun, I thought if I were the NVA, I wouldn't attack us anymore. Our firepower was awesome.

As soon as my shift was over at noon, I grabbed my muddy clothes and boots and walked to the west end of the airstrip where the river was. There was a pleasant sandy beach on the bend of the river, and guys from different units were washing and swimming. There were a few Marines standing ready with M-16s in hand, but there wasn't much chance of a daylight attack. I took a picture of the scene and two of the Golf battery guys before stripping and jumping in the water.

It was the first time I had been able to wash good since the mess hall trip to China Beach. The water was a bit muddy, but very warm. I washed myself first then put on my skivvies and set about washing my boots and utilities. As I was finishing up, one of the guys came out of the water with a leech attached to his leg. His buddy lit a cigarette and touched the lit end to the leech until the little bugger let go. That was the only disadvantage to the river. Leeches were no fun, and if you panicked and pulled it off, the teeth inside the sucker would still be in your body and quickly become infected.

That morning was hot and sunny, and it felt good. It was the kind of morning that made you forget your situation. Just before three in the afternoon, it started raining again. The clouds came on all of a sudden, and it was a downpour. Like everyone else, I could do nothing but protect my camera, rifle, LAW, and ammo with my poncho and sit through it. To make matters worse, we started taking mortars, and a fire mission was called to combat it.

I was off duty and sat in my hole in the mud, fearing the mortars and watching the cannon cockers fire 105mm HE (High Energy) shells to the south side of the main river. It rained so hard that the howitzers dug into the mud, forcing them out of their surveyed position, and the guys were slipping and falling with heavy shells in their hands.

The fire mission stopped because the guns were so out of position that the shells were no longer landing on target. The mortars stopped long before we did, so I felt safe getting up to take a picture. The gun-grunts were tired and muddy, but they were actually laughing at each other's predicament as I took this photo.

So much for washing the mud off. As I started my shift at 4:00 p.m., I was wetter and muddier than I had been that morning. We were informed that we would start four on eight off and have just one chart operator and one computer man a shift. The amtrack was small and we needed men on the line to defend our position. The good thing was having extra replacement FDC guys now and being inside once in awhile. I ate my C-rations half way through the shift, and at 8 pm I went off duty, and Jesse went on. We were staggering shifts and sometimes went longer or shorter depending on the fire missions so sometimes Jesse and I were together and sometimes not. That night we were not together.

During the day we had made bigger fighting holes and had combined holes with others, so that night I was with two other guys and we took turns sleeping in our larger hole. We also had guys go out in the cornfield during the day and dig a series of small LP (listening post) holes a hundred feet out from the wire and about 150 feet apart. There must have been about six of them spread along the south side of the airstrip. Each night one or two men from each unit were required to go outside the perimeter, three to each hole, as a first line of defense.

It was a fitful night sleeping on wet sand bags in a muddy hole. Sometime after midnight I got up and told one of the other guys to try and sleep because I couldn't sleep. I sat there with my back against the mud wall looking at the amtrack and wishing I were inside, warm and dry. As I sat there feeling sorry for myself, I was looking at the guy next to me. He was looking toward the wire, looking and waiting. Then it started. Mortar explosion!

There was no thought of taking cover from mortars as the whole tree line to the south opened up with small arms fire. Remembering the night before, I turned and saw the muzzle flashes of the enemy and started blasting away with my M-16. I have to admit I had a rush of adrenaline, a thrill if you will, and I seemed to thrive on finally being in a small arms firefight. Out of the corner of my eye I could see down the line. A massive amount of firepower was coming from our position. The 50 caliber machine guns on the 155 SPs were blasting and all was a red blur of tracers out-going. I also noticed that the guy with me was huddled down watching me, clutching his M-16. "Let me know if they get close," he said. I nodded, and he said, "I'll help you if they get close." I understood.

The third guy was awake now and firing beside me. I felt a rush as I never had before and kept firing through my second magazine until a bullet whizzed past my head. I didn't need to think about it this time, I knew from personal experience what it was. I stayed down, hearing and feeling the bullets hit the mud above. That lieutenant had wanted firepower, and he got more then he bargained for I'm sure. All of a sudden it was over.

God, I felt great! I wasn't afraid and I felt great! I loved it, the firefight that is, not the mortars. After a while I talked to my hole mate. I asked if he was okay, and he said he was, just shaken a little. He told me he didn't like firing his rifle, but that he would have been there with me if things got worse. I told him I knew he would. Nothing more was said.

After a while of feeling proud of myself, the reality of it all set in, and I realized that I was only happy and proud because no one got hurt bad, especially me. In all that fire only a couple of small wounds were received and no one was in immediate need of a medivac. I couldn't sleep the rest of the night and was actually hoping the NVA would try again. I think the NVA faired worse as the perimeter patrol next morning found areas of blood and body parts in the cornfield. The bodies had been taken away by the NVA.

I was proud of our little artillery force. We fought like grunts for the second time, and we overwhelmed the enemy. That next morning we were all talk, and most guys were like me, telling our individual stories of what happened at our positions and about how much fire we threw at the NVA. I felt for the first time that I now deserved the title, combat veteran, and I would not have to pretend being something I was not. It was a good feeling in light of the situation.

That afternoon and evening went by without incident, and I finished my shift at midnight. Jesse and I were together again, and we stayed in the hole until 2 am waiting for an attack. We finally went to sleep and were awakened by a big explosion. This was not a mortar, and our ears were ringing from it. There was a brief intense firefight, and we joined in, and then all was quiet. We learned that the amtrack had taken a direct hit with an RPG (rocket propelled grenade) that penetrated the 4 inches of steel armor and wounded all inside including our new Lt. V. The thing had gone right over our heads, three feet above the ground. No wonder our ears were ringing. The word was passed to stay in our holes on 100% alert; no one sleeps until daybreak.

When the sun rose and the all clear was given, I got my camera and took pictures of the small hole the RPG made going in and the havoc it released inside. The wounded men, including Lt. V, were medivaced out right after the pictures were taken. Forty-three years later, the man in the next picture, John from Spokane, Washington, and I found each other through a contact at the reunion of

3rd Battalion, 11th Marines, who recognized him in my picture.

That whole day everyone that wasn't on duty helped sandbag the entire amtrack from top to bottom. The coffin was again a scary place to be after we had been reminded of who and what the main target always was. The other Marines respected us FDC guys a little more, because our little group had taken the most causalities since the operation began, including one officer killed and one wounded, and many enlisted men dead and wounded.

After the bagging of the amtrack was finished, I found out that I would have LP duty that night. The line officer met with all of the picked men for that night, and I met the two men I was going to spend the night with. The officer gave us the protocol for the holes including the rule about only one man sleeping and two awake at all times. We had a landline phone and were to check its working order every half hour if not called sooner. If we were engaged in enemy contact or saw the enemy first, we were to stay low and start the firefight. Then after the rest of our guys took over, we were to remain low in the hole so as not to get shot by our own men behind us. We were not to talk unless it was on the phone. We were not to get out of the hole or stand for any reason until called back in the morning. That meant pissing in the hole or out the sidewall of the hole without standing up. We were not to call out; corpsman would not be available to us. In other words we were not to do anything to give away our position after we entered it.

We then walked out to the holes in the cornfield and checked out the one we were going to defend. Mine, of course, was directly out from the FDC amtrack where the attack started last night. My bravery of the other night diminished into fear once again. This was not going to be fun. Before we returned to the perimeter I noticed some ears of corn on the stocks around the hole. They were very small, but after peeling one, I noticed they were yellow and ripe.

I picked a half dozen ears and took them back for dinner. I made a fire with canned heat, some scrap wood, and a few pellets of C-2 from leftover powder bags, and boiled up the small ears in a metal pot the amtrack driver kept in the vehicle. That was quite a good dinner. The corn, even without butter, was sweet and tasty.

About an hour after dark the LP guys met and went over the briefing again. The word was passed down the line, as it did every night that the listening post guys were going out to set up their ambushes. My two companions and I left the wire at our marked place and walked straight out, counting our steps to find the hole. We were off by about 15 feet to the left, but there was enough starlight to find it easily. We settled in without saying a word, and since I had radio experience, they both wanted me to work the phone. I called in to let the line officer know we were in position and ready.

For the first three hours no one slept. We were scared to death. It was the second time for one of the guys, and he whispered a few words of encouragement to the third guy and me. We sat and looked and looked and listened. Every shadow was a potential target. Every so often a pop flare would shoot up like a Roman candle, and we would cower down so as not to make ourselves seen by the enemy. The light from those parachute flares was surreal. We thought a live enemy body would appear out of the cornstalks at any moment. I had never done anything so scary in my life. Thoughts of John Wayne and "The Sands of Iwo Jima" ran through my head.

I thought of dying in that hole with those two guys I didn't know. What a shitty death that would be. A little later I tried to sleep but was too afraid, and I wanted to be ready to fire when the attack came. It was the longest night of my life up until that time.

Why we were never attacked that night, I'll never know, but I think it might have been because of the heavy fire of the last three nights. As the sun rose we were called back, and I faintly heard the word pass down the line, "LP's coming in. Hold your fire."

Those of us on LP duty got to sleep all day. I ate breakfast and slept until afternoon when I went to the river to clean up and wash clothes. The next night and day we took no incoming, and the word was that the 7th Marines were clearing the NVA out of the valley. The following day I was assigned to guard duty at one of the 30 caliber machine gun emplacements.

We were to take up our positions well before dark. Mine was next to one of the tanks that came and went because the 7th Marines needed them. I met with the machine gunner and his helper and one other guy like me who was to provide cover fire. The gunner gave us a quick refresher lesson in case we needed to take his place, and we settled in for the night.

An hour later, when it was dusk, the first mortars landed sending everyone into action. We waited, looking for the muzzle flashes in the tree line when a mortar landed next our position. Our machine gun nest had a corrugated metal and sand bag roof over it, and when the round hit, a sand bag fell down in front of me hitting the barrel of my M-16. I was in position to fire so the butt of my M-16 was under my chin. The sand bag was heavy and when it hit the tip of my barrel, the butt hit me under the chin knocking me back. Falling back, I was dazed, and the machine gunner thought I was shot. He called for the corpsman before I could tell him I was okay.

The corpsman was running through the mortar fire and jumped into the nest with us. He was pissed when he found out I wasn't hurt.

"You mean I ran over here for nothing?" he yelled. "Next time make sure there is blood coming out from somewhere!" Then he left just before the small arms fire started.

The guys in the tank were shooting their 50 cal. and we were shooting the 30 cal. at the tree line directly in front of us when the tankers got a call on the radio. I could hear the tank commander scream at his guys to get back to the tank because their brother tank was down the road a half-mile and under attack. The tank started and those four guys jumped in. Off they flew right over the cornfield into the enemy fire, turned left when they hit the road, and sped away. The firefight stopped then. I think the NVA in front of us thought the tank was coming after them because they stopped firing and took off. About fifteen minutes later both tanks returned, and we had a restful, peaceful night.

During the few weeks we were at the airstrip, there were few opportunities for mail. One morning I was lucky enough to be picked to go back to Hill 55 by Sea Knight and bring back the mail. I boarded a re-supply chopper around 11:00 a.m. and headed back to Hill 55. I was the only passenger, and twenty minutes later we were landing. The crew chief said we would be leaving in twenty minutes and to be right back because they would not wait for me once they were loaded.

I left the Sea Knight carrying my M-16 and started up to 3rd Battalion HQ tent. I know other Marines were watching me because I was so dirty. This time I didn't have to pretend to be a combat vet, and those guys, especially the office Marines in the HQ tent, knew where I had come from and where I was returning to. I reached the tent and recognized no one. I walked in and said I was here for the Thuong Duc mail and all four typewriters stopped for a beat. They all looked up and looked at me, then three of them returned to typing. They looked like they were back in the states. Their boots were even polished. The one clerk handed me a big red canvas mailbag with a lock on the zipper and I took it. I waited a second, but none of them said anything to me so I turned and left with the bag. No how are you, how you doing? They just lowered their heads and typed.

Returning to the Sea Knight I sat and watched as the loading of the ammo was finished. One of the Marines loading came over to me and sat down.

"Going back out there?" he said.

"Yeah," I responded.

"Where to?" he asked.

"Thuong Duc," I replied.

"Man," he said as he turned his head, "that's the shits," and he walked away.

I squeezed into the Sea Knight and sat on ammo boxes for the return flight. As always, every one crowded around the mailbag when someone appeared with it and this time was no exception. Mail was always good.

By now it was around the fifteenth of June 1968, and we had not had any enemy contact for a couple of days. I was sitting in my hole in the afternoon when we got word that we were going back to Hill 10, close to DaNang, Golf battery's home base. Our mission was over for now, and the 7th Marines had driven the NVA back into the mountains. I looked up at the Special Forces Camp above the river and village less than a quarter mile away and pondered their fate. I knew the Green Berets were back because they had visited our position on the airstrip from time to time. I was sure glad we were leaving. I had my combat experience, my stories to tell, and was eager to get back into a secure bunker at Hill 10. I soon learned that I would be promoted to Corporal E-4 as of July 1st, my second combat promotion, and that I was permanently assigned to Golf battery now. The amtrack and the 155 SPs were staying to support the 7th Marines who were keeping at least one company in the area to support the Green Beret A-Team.

I remember that as I was packing things up, I was reflecting on my time here and being thankful it wasn't worse. For the most part, casualties were light except for us at the FDC and were not too bad for the 7th Marines either. We boarded the trucks late in the morning and headed back out of the Thuong Duc Valley toward Hill 65 and India battery. The trip went fast as there was no contact with NVA, and we passed Hill 65 sometime after noon.

About half way to Hill 55, at a place called Dai Loc, we passed a long straight stretch of rice paddies with a tree line about a quarter of a mile away. All of a sudden the center of our convoy took small arms fire from the tree line. I remember it almost being a nuisance firefight. We were battle hardened now, and even though we were artillery, we took no more shit from anyone. A good portion of the column opened up on the tree line with our

M-16s, and the firepower was heavy from our end. The NVA, or VC, obviously wanted no part of us; they probably thought we were supply trucks with just drivers and shotguns.

Without missing a beat we passed the area, drove another half mile and called in a strike. We watched five minutes later as Marine F-4s were dropping five hundred pound bombs on the area. Satisfied, our officers continued on to Hill 55 where Jesse and I and the other newer FDC replacements were dropped off to collect the rest of our personal gear and sea bags. A truck would pick us up the next day for the ride to Hill 10.

That night the other Thuong Duc vets and I were the talk of 3rd Battalion HQ, and I hit the mess hall first with my plastic quart pitcher in hand. I went directly to the milk machine and ice cream tubs and filled that thing to the top. After nothing but C-rations for the last 30 plus days, I was eager for real food. After the ice cream I waited an hour and then had dinner, my first hot food in a long while. I don't remember what it was, but it must have been good.

After dinner I returned to the FDC bunker where I met old friends and told my stories. Lt. C was there and so was Sgt. L, and after checking on my cot and gear in the FDC hooch, we headed to the small enlisted men's tent where cold beer was the featured fare. It was the first time in Vietnam that I drank beer enough to get tipsy, but I felt it was an appropriate occasion.

I felt safe and secure going to sleep that night on Hill 55, with my rubber air mattress, sheets and a blanket. What a change from the mud, mortars, and firefights. I thought about all these HQ guys who would never experience what Jesse and I had been through. I felt pride in what we had done. We were basically a bunch of kids with new college graduates leading us. A year before none of us had any military knowledge. It boggled my mind. I slept well.

Next morning we had a big breakfast of eggs and bacon and milk. We packed our gear and waited for the truck. The ride to Hill 10 was as uneventful as we assumed it would be, and we arrived at the hill before noon mess. We checked into the FDC hooch, and I set up a nice cubicle for myself.

I could almost see DaNang from our hill. It wasn't as high as Hill 55, but it was a lot closer to Da Nang and relative safety. We were situated at the east end of Charlie Ridge, and although this was by no means a safe place, I felt better than at Thuong Duc. The FDC bunker was roomy and someone had the smarts enough to make it bigger so that three 2x4 wooden bunk beds were built into one wall. We had six bunks for when we were being mortared, and the off duty guys could sleep safely down there. I liked it. I felt safe. I was happy here with Golf battery and Hill 10.

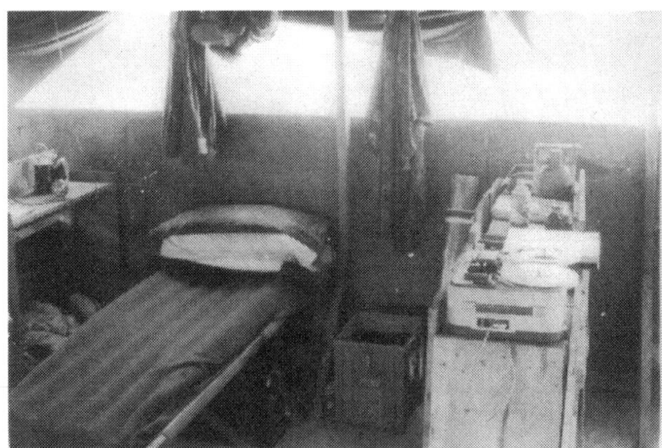

HANK IN DANANG

The next week passed quickly and my mail finally caught up with me again. My high school buddy, Hank, who was a year in the Corps ahead of me, wrote me from DaNang where his motor transport unit was stationed. Hank was a truck driver, and he invited me to come see him if I could get there. Now, I had heard of these reunions of friends before, so I went to my new FDC sergeant who had not been with us at Thuong Duc and showed him the letter. He was receptive, and since things had been quiet and since I was now a corporal, he said I could catch a ride with a truck leaving in the morning.

I was up early next morning and had another good breakfast at the Hill 10 mess hall. It was smaller than Hill 55's and didn't always have ice cream, my mainstay, but I remember the food being better. I caught a ride with a truck driver who knew the unit I was looking for. He said he could take me to their front door. It wasn't yet 8:00 a.m. and we were waiting for the roads to be cleared of mines. He asked me if I wanted to ride in the seat up front, but I declined saying I would rather ride in back where, if anything happened, I could give him cover fire. He looked at me like I was crazy. I told him I had just done that a week ago coming back from Thuong Duc Valley. He didn't seem impressed, but it was true. I couldn't fire effectively inside the cab, and I wanted to be able to if the situation presented itself.

I climbed up on the truck, locked and loaded outside of the gate, and we left the Hill 10 compound. Speeding toward 1st Tanks, our first checkpoint about a mile and a half away, I enjoyed the warm morning. The wind was blowing my hair as I rode standing up behind the cab with my helmet off. Four minutes later we were waved through 1st Tanks compound, and ten minutes after that we reached the DaNang checkpoint.

We were waved through again, and we wound through the narrow streets full of trucks, jeeps, and Vietnamese people going every which way. A short time later the driver pulled off to the side of the road just past a gated compound. He stepped out and told me I was at the place I was looking for, and sure enough, the sign on the gate confirmed it. I thanked him, and he wished me luck.

Jumping down off the truck I approached the MP guard and told him who I was looking for. He told me to check in at unit HQ and then let me pass by. He reminded me to clear my weapon. It took me back for a second, but he was right. I took my M-16 and removed the magazine and ejected the round in the chamber. He said they should have told me to clear my M-16 at the main DaNang checkpoint. I told him I was sorry and that I should have realized it. I also said I wasn't used to coming into DaNang. He said he understood.

I continued to the HQ hut and, as luck would have it, Hank's unit was still doing morning maintenance on their trucks and had not left the compound yet. The Gsgt. was nice, and he sent a PFC after Hank, and the two of them returned shortly. Hank and I hugged and shook each other; it was so good to see him. He noticed my corporal chevrons and was surprised. I said it wasn't official until July1, another three days, but everyone knew it back at Hill 10.

"I've been in almost two years," he said, "and I just turned E-4 a couple of months ago."

"I know," I said, "but they promote faster out where I am." I told him of the dead and wounded we sustained the last month in my unit, and that I was doing a sergeant's job. I told the brief story of Thuong Duc to Hank and his sergeant, and then the sergeant told Hank to take the day off and show me the sights.

Hank got a jeep and we spent the day going all over DaNang. He showed me the big PX, and we had hamburgers and hotdogs for lunch. He took me to where Bob Hope had done his Christmas show and many other places. The day went fast and it was getting later in the afternoon when Hank took me back to the DaNang check point. He waited with me until a truck headed for 1st Tanks came by and stopped at the checkpoint. I thought maybe I could have a better chance catching a truck to Hill 10 from there. After Hank and I shook hands and said our goodbyes, I climbed on the truck and we took off in a cloud of dust.

The drive to 1st Tanks didn't take long, and I jumped off the truck and headed for the check point HQ. I let the guards know where I was going, and they said a truck might still come by. I waited an hour; it was now 4:30 p.m. and I was due back at 6:00 p.m. when they closed the wire. I asked the guard shack if they had a radio frequency for Golf battery Hill 10, and they said their radio only connected to 1st Tanks HQ and 26th Marines.

I asked the Marine guards how much enemy activity they had the last few days, and they said they'd had none between them and Hill 10 for some time. It was 4:45 p.m. and I had to make a decision. It was a mile and a half to Hill 10, an easy twenty-five minute walk for me. I asked the guards if I was crazy to walk it this time of day. They said the odds were with me if I chose to try it. They also said if I went now and got into trouble, they would hear the fire from my M-16 and come running. After 6 pm curfew I was on my own.

I didn't want to be late or worse, AWOL, so I struck out at a brisk pace. "Wish me luck," I laughed to the guards, but deep inside I wasn't sure I was making a good choice. I could see the rocket tower on Hill 10 and that gave me courage, but fifteen minutes into the walk and I was sure I had made a mistake. I was glad I had my helmet and flak jacket, as I almost didn't take them that morning.

Up ahead was a small village of half dozen hooches, and as I approached, a farmer in the rice paddy stopped his water buffalo and watched me. I half turned to stare at him with my meanest stare, but continued on. In the middle of the village, I surprised some kids, and they ran away inside a hooch.

Ten seconds later another man appeared out of the last hooch in front of me. He was startled to see me and he was unarmed, but I pulled back on my bolt rod and made like I had just put a round in the chamber, although I already had one in, just to freeze him. Our eyes locked, and although he didn't seem unfriendly, he respected my M-16 and didn't move for fear I would shoot him.

I turned and half walked backward for a full minute, keeping my eyes on the village as the women and kids came back outside to watch me go. I then stopped, smiled, and waved to them in a feeble attempt to show them I meant them no harm. I turned and hurried along. I looked back every few paces to check my back trail, and soon I was around the next bend and out of sight. Then I ran.

The most beautiful sight I had seen all day was Hill 10 less than a quarter of a mile away. I didn't care who saw me, I was scared now and I doubled timed for a couple of minutes. I slowed down as the compound gate neared and slowed to a leisurely walk. As I got closer, the two Marine guards saw me and got up weapons drawn. I was sure they knew I was a Marine, and just as sure they couldn't believe their eyes. I slowed even more and as I came abreast of them.

I said, "Golf battery, FDC."

"Where the hell did you come from?" the first one asked.

"1st Tanks," I replied. "I was seeing a friend in DaNang."

"Are you crazy or stupid?" the second one said.

"Nobody would mess with me in daylight," was my cocky response as I cleared my weapon.

I wasn't shaking visibly, but I was inside, and I hoped they bought my cockiness. They watched me walk up the hill. I vowed to myself to never do that again.

RETURN TO THUONG DUC

After reporting in at the FDC, I was told to get some dinner and be ready for the 8:00 a.m. to noon shift tomorrow. I effectively had twenty-four hours off. Earlier in the week some of us had built a shower like I had seen on Hill 55, and I hadn't had a chance to use it yet. So since I had the night off, I decided to take a shower, put on some brand new underwear I had bought at the PX in DaNang, and sleep on my cot and rubber air mattress outside the hooch under the stars.

The shower was an old 55-gallon drum with a wooden stopper turned upside down in a wooden frame. The barrel was filled from five-gallon water cans carried from the water purification tank. The heat from the sun heated the water, and luckily it had been filled and still had some hot water left inside. I asked around, and the guys that filled it had already had their showers, so no one minded if I used it. I said I would re-fill it in the morning.

The water was clean, unlike the river at Thuong Duc, and the hot water felt good. We took shipboard showers, meaning we got wet, stopped the water, soaped up, and then rinsed, not letting the water run too long. The soaping up was the best, as we had no soap on operation. I hadn't been this clean since the last time I used the shower on Hill 55 over two months ago.

That night I enjoyed my time off. I lay on my cot and looked south to the Arizona Bad Lands country and watched a lone "Puff the Magic Dragon" spit red tracers down on the enemy many miles away. Every so often a few green and red tracers would fly up toward Puff, but they slowed way down before they reached him. Puff was a Douglas AC-47, WWII era plane, with a mighty big gun. It would circle a target pouring concentrated fire on the enemy. Watching at night was most exciting.

After an hour of watching Puff and contemplating my life to that point in time, I fell into a deep, restful sleep. The next morning and the few days that followed were uneventful except for a cobra snake we found outside our hooch one day. We weren't too happy about letting it roam freely, so armed with 2x4 boards, we beat it to death. We also captured and killed rats and mice running around the bunker with trap cages, and we kept a running KIA total of the flies we killed. I can't remember who killed the most flies.

Life was bearable until the morning of July 3rd, 1968. It had only been two weeks and a couple of days since leaving Thuong Duc, and now I found myself listening to the FDC sergeant telling me I was going back out to Thuong Duc with a four man FDC crew, guns 5 and 6 from Golf battery, and their corresponding Marine gunners to support the 7th Marines and the Green Beret A-Team again. Seems that since Golf left, things had gotten worse.

Jesse was there, and he volunteered to go, too. The sergeant said that Jesse and I were the two best FDC men he had, and one of us had to stay with the battery on Hill 10. Jesse offered to go and let me stay. I said nothing, waiting to see what the sarge would say. He told Jesse the order came from higher up; there was nothing he could do to change it.

Jesse was disappointed, and I know why. He was as good as me, but they picked me, and he knew why they picked me. The best man always got the hardest, most dangerous job, and Jesse knew they thought I was better. I knew I wasn't any better; I was just older and white. That little Mexican had more courage in one hand than I had all together. I had the utmost respect for him, and at the moment when I turned to leave, prior to getting my things ready, I wanted to tell him so, but I couldn't find the words. I've regretted that for forty-three years.

I really wanted to trade places with him, but I could never say that in front those I was about to take back out to Thuong Duc. Only one of the other guys had been there before. The other three were new replacements. As it turned out, I never saw Jesse again. I hope he stayed on Hill 10 and survived the war.

That morning I boarded a Sea Knight and headed for Thuong Duc for the second time, and this time the CH-46 landed on the Special Forces camp LZ above the river and village. The hill was a horseshoe shaped plateau, with steep sides in all directions, except an end finger to a high ridge running west toward Laos.

The A-Team and their South Vietnamese Rangers occupied the north and west side. The entrance road was in the middle of the east side and sloped at a good angle down to the village. We Marines were to occupy the road and south side up above the sheer cliff that fell away to the Song Vu Gia River below. At least we wouldn't have to worry about that path of attack. It was a shear cliff.

The lieutenant that was with us and I began surveying in the gun positions while the other guys made an FDC defensive position for the night located with the cliff top at our back. They used a wide, deep existing ditch and sand bags, and it was big enough for the six of us. As we continued to survey, I kept looking for the two 105 howitzers, guns five and six, and their men, to fly in any second. It was getting late and it would be dark soon. They never came.

As it got dark I had a very bad feeling. This was to be my second most scary night in Vietnam. There were only six of us on that whole south side of the hill, and the lieutenant said that the Green Berets would have some of their Rangers manning the wire and ditches protecting the western and eastern flank.

"This is great," I thought. "Only six of us with no water, except that amount still in our canteens, no food, one PRC 25 radio and very little ammo. Less than 100 rounds per man." We thought the guns would come with us, and with them all the supplies for our new Golf Forward battery. Not that night. And to top it off we were fronted by a bunch of Vietnamese Rangers who we wouldn't be able to tell from the NVA after it got dark. The lieutenant chose to stay a few meters away in another hole. Needless to say, the rest of us stayed in our big hole and slept uneasily all night.

We had finished the survey of the gun emplacements before dark, before we went to the defensive hole. I turned on the radio and, for the first of many times, used my new call sign to check in with 3rd Battalion HQ.

"Hireling, this is Hireling Golf Forward, radio check over," I said.

A longer than normal pause ensued, and I called in again. Another long pause and then a response.

"Hireling Golf forward, this is Hireling. We have you loud and clear. Sorry about the wait.

Wasn't sure I heard you right. Hadn't heard of you before. Needed confirmation. Out."

Well, there we were: hungry, thirsty, and scared. Those radiomen at HQ knew us now, and they knew where we were by now. They were probably counting their blessings they weren't out here with us, and I was getting more afraid by the minute.

We passed the early evening talking about where we would go on R&R. We had all heard stories about R&R, and since I had the most time in country, the guys were interested in where I was planning to go. I had already put in for September 1st for Bangkok, Thailand. I had picked Bangkok because it was a short flight and I wanted the most time possible with the young ladies I expected to meet.

When you're sitting in a mud hole in the middle of a war, most guys have a hard time telling lies like they did back in high school. I personally had one dreadful sexual experience in a car with an older girl I didn't love or know or even care about. It was awful.

Most of the guys were eighteen and complete virgins so it shouldn't be surprising that we all were looking forward to R & R. Some of the guys talked about how one place had better girls than other places, and some guys wanted to get a different girl every night. I have to admit it was a major reason we all had in staying alive. After a few hours of boy talk in the darkness, we took turns trying to sleep.

Luckily the night passed without incident and the rest of Golf Forward battery started arriving early next morning. We soon were eating C-rations and drinking out of five-gallon cans of fresh water. We spent the day unloading choppers and filling sand bags. By the end of the second day, I felt safer with two 105s and two dozen Marines around a circular perimeter enclosing the guns and FDC hole. The Rangers would continue to protect our western flank throughout the next two months.

SETTLING IN FOR THE LONG HAUL

It was obvious by the third day that we needed a better way of filling sand bags. Thuong Duc Special Forces Camp was one big rock. The ground was so hard that we could barely break into it. The previous day had not only brought our two 105s, but two 2.5 ton trucks and a jeep. Someone got the bright idea to take a truck down to the river to the sand bar where we were swimming a month ago, and fill the sand bags there. What a lifesaver.

About eight of us took one of the trucks the 300-meter drive down to the river sand bar. The truck had a cab turret mounted with a 50-caliber machine gun, and we all had our M-16s. One guy sat up at the 50, and one guy was ready with his M-16. The rest of us began filling sand bags. It was so easy.

Within minutes we began attracting kids of all ages and sizes. At first we tried to chase them away, but they kept coming back. A month ago the 7th Marines kept the sand bar free of any villagers, but we didn't have the manpower, so we gave up trying. These kids were good kids, and their parents were good mountain people. They were more afraid of the NVA than we were. I decided to engage these kids as friends and started taking their pictures. Part of our mission here was supposed to be the winning over of the local population so the guys of Golf Forward began a six-week relationship with the Thuong Duc kids.

We continued filling the sand bags and continued interacting with the kids with smiles and funny faces, and before long the older boys began helping us. They took the E-tools from us and soon none of us were filling sand bags, we were just hoisted them up into the truck bed.

I knew we had to offer payment at some point, but all we had were cigarettes and the C-rations we brought along for lunch. I wasn't a smoker and hated smokes, so I encouraged the guys to pay with our lunch instead. The boys loved the C-rations, and I was hoping they would take the cigarettes to their dads.

We made a second trip in the afternoon, and this time we had more food for payment. We also had some South Vietnamese Rangers with us, one of which spoke some English, and we could communicate better with the kids.

The boys dug right into the work, but the girls stayed back at a distance. The boys were hard workers, and we took the opportunity to wash and swim a little in the river while the boys filled sand bags. Before long they had a huge pile of filled bags, and I got them all together on the bags, had them salute, and snapped a picture.

The boys were great, and soon each of us had a favorite kid that took care of us by washing our boots and clothes while we bathed in the river. I had one kid in particular named Donn that became my adopted boy. We were best of friends whenever I came to the river, which was a lot. He always wore a white pith helmet and I found out his dad was the town barber. He was a good kid. I hope he survived the war.

We came to the river every day that first week, and all the sand bags and the empty 105 boxes filled with sand were transforming the camp into a formidable defensive position. Some of the Rangers would come too, but instead of sandbags, they would make bricks. The Green Berets must have gotten a load of cement for the Rangers to make their bricks.

By the end of the first week our side of the camp was shaping up. We had good sized bunkers for the FDC and a couple bunkers for each gun crew made out of 105 ammo boxes filled with sand and sandbags. We laid out more wire and laid Claymore mines. We had a 55-gallon drum, cut in half, flown in for use as our shitter, and some engineers showed up with a canvas water purification pool so we could purify the river water. We also had the four 155 SPs move up the hill from the old French airstrip and things looked mighty different than they had a week before.

Not all our time was a swim in the river and good times. At night we took mortars from time to time, and the NVA would test our western flank on occasion. The Rangers did their job, as we never had the compound breached by sappers. We also shot lots of fire missions every night and a few daylight missions. We had so many 105 spent brass shell casings that it was getting hard to stack them. We never had any daylight firefights so things became very easy while the sun was up. At night we slept on top of the FDC bunker on rubber air mattresses that were brought in from Hill 55 supply.

The South China Sea was twenty-five miles away, and I would lie on the bunker at night and see Puff from the air, and firefights, and ambushes on the ground. My night view commanded the whole coastal plain from Da Nang to Tam Ky, and there was almost never a time when I didn't see tracers somewhere. At times, watching the tracers seemed beautiful until I came back to reality and remembered that someone was being wounded or killed.

I can't remember much about the lieutenant we had at first; he kept to himself, but after the second week an old friend, Lt. C, was transferred out from Hill 55 to us on temporary assignment. It was good being with him again, and we talked often while he was there.

One night while Lt. C and I were on duty in our small FDC bunker, we got a fire mission from one of the A-Team members on patrol far to the west of us in NVA territory. Their recon squad was engaged and surrounded by the enemy, and they had no way out. Their plan was to call in 105 fire from us, just to east of their position, and in the confusion make a break and fight their way back to Thuong Duc.

The fire mission was danger close, which meant that the adjusting round would be within 50 meters of the man calling it in. Gun five fired a round and the Green Beret squad leader called back an adjustment and fire for effect. I made the change and Lt. C checked it. We radioed the gun crews for six rounds on the new data. Six rounds went out and the Green Beret radioed back, "Repeat fire for effect." This time he left his handset on and we heard our rounds land. We heard small arms fire as well.

The squad tried to move, but the engagement became critical. The Green Beret radioed back that his squad of Rangers had dead and wounded. We could hear the battle sounds as he spoke. He called in another round of fire, and this time were heard him scream. After a long pause we looked at each other in the FDC and wondered the worst. The Green Beret came back on the radio. His voice was garbled, and he was wounded bad; he told us his situation was hopeless and called for another six rounds on his position. We never heard from him again.

The next morning, as soon as it was light, Lt. C went to the A-Team side of the hill to ask about their man. All we ever heard was that they would send a recon team to try and find his body. Over the next few weeks until we were pulled out, we never heard anything more. The experience bothered us all, especially Lt. C. He was depressed and felt it was somehow his fault. We all felt that way; those of us who listened to the radio that night and could do nothing to help this man and his Ranger squad. It was nobody's fault, but we all felt the hurt.

As the days went by I seemed to become less concerned with my safety, and knowing that Thuong Duc Special Forces Camp was a big target and that the NVA were all around us didn't seem to matter anymore. I took daylight trips into the village from time to time, walking or riding in our one jeep. Usually two or three of us went and most of the time I took pictures.

One particular time I had a drawing notebook and a pencil, and when we stopped in the center of the village, the kids swarmed around us as usual. This time I stayed in the jeep and drew cartoons of Mickey Mouse and Donald Duck for the kids and gave a copy to everyone who wanted one. One of my FDC guys who was with me took my camera and snapped a picture.

Many of my Marine friends who in later years saw this picture wondered why I was wearing a black beret. One said the only time he saw a black beret was on Tom Selleck's character, Magnum PI, in the old TV series. Tom wore a black beret in his Vietnam scenes.

My beret has a simple explanation. Some of the South Vietnamese Rangers wore black or camouflage berets, and after making friends with one of them that spoke English, we were able to trade cigarettes for fresh corn and bananas. One day I traded for a black beret that was too big for my friend, and I wore it at Thuong Duc most days. Of course it was not standard Marine issue, but we hardly ever had any brass on our hill other than a lieutenant once in a while. The other guys usually never wore any cover at all, or for that matter, any shirts either. Dress codes on our hill were lax.

Dress codes reminds me of a situation that occurred on Hill 55 when I made my one and only mail run in August. I had just left the LZ on Hill 55 and headed for the Battalion office hut. It was late in the morning and the place was stirring with activity. Up the dirt road ahead of me, I noticed two, brand new, shiny 2nd lieutenants walking toward me, and seeing as how I needed to be on the other side of the road when I got to the HQ hut anyway, I crossed early to avoid saluting the officers. I guess my body language gave me away, because they called me on it.

"Corporal," one lieutenant called, "come over here."

I stopped, looked at them, and pointed a finger at myself. "Me?" As if I didn't know.

"Yes, you, the dirty one," he replied.

I thought, "Shit, now I have to play Marine with these assholes." I turned and walked over to them. Now, we never saluted our officers in the field, but some still considered Hill 55 a stateside hill.

"Yes, sir," I said when I got to them.

"Aren't you forgetting something, corporal?" the second one asked.

Well, I knew what these assholes wanted, so I came to attention and saluted. I did my best to animate my movements and this pissed them off a little more.

"Are you trying to be smart, corporal?" the first one demanded.

"No, sir," I said. Yes, of course I was!

"I can see why you tried to avoid us," the second one said. "You're a mess. Don't you ever clean your utilities?"

"What's your name and unit, corporal?" the first one asked.

Now I was pissed. Here I am getting mortared and shot at on a regular basis, and these two want me on report.

"Sir, I'm here for my unit's mail," I said. "My name is Corporal Cowart, my call-sign is Hireling Golf Forward, my unit is Golf Forward battery, 3rd Battalion, 11th Marines, located twenty miles due west of here at Thuong Duc Special Forces Camp on the Laotian border. Since my lieutenant isn't located on this Hill, I suggest you talk to the Major. He knows who I am, …sir."

Thuong Duc wasn't that close to the Laotian border, but I could see this impressed the two second lieutenants, and I noticed that they had nothing to write with so all this bullshit would be for nothing.

"Is there anything more, sir?" I continued, "I have a CH-46 waiting for me on the LZ."

It took a second for them to respond.

"Just try and get a better attitude, corporal, and salute officers instead of avoiding them."

"Yes, sir," I responded. I saluted sharply, did an about face, (it was the only about face I remember doing in Vietnam) and walked away without looking back. I got the mail and returned to the LZ. The lieutenants were nowhere in sight, and I never heard anything more about it. When I returned to Thuong Duc, I let everyone know what happened, warning them to watch out for the new lieutenants.

As the first long days of August passed by, we shot more and more fire missions, mostly at night, and took less incoming mortars. We had some new replacements and a new lieutenant.

Lt. L was a Seattle boy like me, and we talked some of home, but I could tell that he was uncomfortable around enlisted men. He wasn't a snob or uptight; he just kept up that officer wall so you couldn't get close to him.

We also got two new FDC guys. One was to become my closest friend in Vietnam even though we only knew each other three weeks. The other was a young, maybe less than eighteen, kid Marine with an attitude.

In my six months in Vietnam I had never seen a younger looking Marine in the FDC. When I first approached this kid, I wanted to make him feel welcome in what I was sure was an uncomfortable surrounding. I wanted to be the good corporal to this Marine, but he complained about everything. I even had him come with us when we took a truck down to the river for a swim and wash.

Since he was new, I assigned him to watch the guns and the truck first, and then he could take a swim later. He was not happy about this, and he made a comment. I ignored his words because he was new, but I gave him my mean look while telling him to keep the kids away from the truck and our rifles.

I wasn't in the water two minutes when I heard a burst of M-16 fire and bullets hitting the water. The other guys and I ducked for cover and began running naked out of the water thinking we were under attack. Very quickly it became apparent that our new, young Marine was the cause of the rifle fire.

I saw him standing there with an M-16 in his hands, yelling at the kids who had congregated at the sand bar as usual. I walked over to the truck, forgetting I was naked.

"What the f*** you think you're doing?" I screamed. "What the hell are you shooting at the kids for?"

"You told me to keep them away," he replied.

"I didn't tell you to shoot them!" It was then I noticed the M-16 he so leisurely held in his hands.

Like mother penguins and their babies, a Marine comes to know his own rifle at a distance even though they look the same as every one else's. This guy was holding *my* M-16! I was really pissed now.

"That's my f***ing M-16!" I yelled. "You fired my rifle, asshole!"

"I just grabbed the nearest one," he said.

"Who's going to clean my rifle?" I bellowed.

"I'll clean the damn thing, big f***ing deal."

"Damn right you will! Give that to me." He handed me my M-16, and I went back over to where my clothes were piled to get my pants back on. "Everyone! Get back in the truck," I yelled. "We're going back before they send someone to see what the shooting was about."

I grabbed my stuff and everyone piled onto the truck bed. I gave the young kid another dirty look and told the driver to get moving.

The young kid stared back at me. "I said I'd clean your rifle," he said. "What's the big deal?"

I looked at him again. "On second thought, you won't have time to clean it."

All during this exchange no one else had said anything, only the two of us. It was quiet on the drive back up the hill and as soon as we pulled to a stop, I got out and found Lt. L. I told the lieutenant what had happened.

"He did what?" Lt. L asked incredulously.

"You heard me right, sir. Either that kid gets on the next chopper out of here or I will!" I said. "We can't have trigger happy assholes like him out here. He's gonna kill one of us."

"Settle down, Corporal Cowart. He's gone. Get him out of here."

In less than an hour the young Marine was on his way back to Hill 55 and probably some discipline.

After things settled down, I took the other new replacement, John, off to the side and talked with him.

"I assume you're not going to give me trouble like the other one that just left."

"No," John said in his slow Southern California way. "I don't even like shooting my M-16."

By the end of the night John and I were best of friends. We stayed that way until we left the hill for good, never seeing one another again.

One day John and one of the other FDC guys started this crazy way of talking with an Italian accent. Before long everyone on the hill was speaking like he just got off the boat from Italy and had just learned English. John even grew a goatee to look more Italian.

"Hey, giva me the salta, woulda youa please, sa."

"I giva you a swifta kick ina you ass-a-hole-a, insteada."

And so it went night and day. Some times we would do it on radio checks with battalion, and they would come back with, "Hireling Golf Forward, please use standard radio procedure, out."

It was stupid, but it was fun and it kept our spirits up in slack times. And slack times were beginning to become rare.

The second week of August saw things heat up a bit, and I don't mean the weather. We were taking more incoming, and the 7th Marine platoons that patrolled around us were getting more contact.

About that time one 7th Marine platoon came on the hill for a night, as they often did, to catch a break. We always had them stay on the cliff side so most of them could sleep all night without worry. This particular platoon, like most Marine infantry platoons, had a heavy concentration of black Marines. Two black grunts in particular settled in near the FDC bunker, and since I was off duty, I was watching them settle in, and I was pointing out the shitter, the water purifying tank and other bright spots about the hill I thought they should know.

They were obviously best of friends and continually joked with one another in ghetto slang that was enjoyable to hear. They had a close bond.

John and I were starting our evening meal of beans and franks in a C-ration can as the two black Marines were beginning to clean their rifles. I was looking right at them and smiling at their good-natured verbal jabs to one another. All of a sudden the Marine on the right set the butt of his M-16 down on the ground, not harder than usual. Again, I was looking right at him so I know his rifle bolt was open, which it should have been after you clear your weapon. As he set the rifle butt down, the bolt snapped shut and the rifle fired.

It was the worst thing that could happen to a Marine. The instructors went over it again and again in boot camp, ITR, and staging battalion. But life has its twists of reality and sometimes the extractor on the bolt of a rifle doesn't work properly and a round is left in the chamber.

As I said, I was looking right at it so I know the first black Marine had attempted to clear his rifle, but the round left in his chamber exploded into the neck of his best friend.

It took me a moment to understand what I had just seen. The second black Marine fell immediately and his best friend started screaming. I ran over along with many others and yelled for a corpsman. Two showed up very quickly. The man's blood was everywhere, his carotid artery obviously severed. The corpsman tried to stop the bleeding, and a call went out for a medivac chopper.

The first black Marine was on his knees crying. I felt so bad for him. I wanted to do something, but what could I do? What could any of us do? We all stood around watching the life of a young man fade away. Who knows what kind of man he would have been? What kind of husband, father, friend. And I was heartbroken for the first black Marine. He couldn't stop crying. He kept saying, “I killed him, I killed him,” over and over and over again.

At least his captain had the good sense to send the man and his squad leader back with the body. The first black Marine would have been of no further use to himself or his platoon if they left him out here.

I was seized with hatred for Thuong Duc. I hated this hill, I hated this war, I hated all the rich college protesters back home, and I hated the athletes with their medical deferments. I hated everything that night.

I couldn’t imagine how many North Vietnamese I had help kill with artillery, and how their friends and family cried over them.

Above all I hated the politicians on both sides who didn’t have to lie in the mud and get shot at. I hated their children who were safe at home, and I hated the owners of munitions factories who were making tons of money off this war while our blood commingled with the red Vietnamese dirt.

–

I got over it. For the time being. I had a job to do and the guns still had to fire. That evening we fired into the early morning hours and the grunts didn't get much sleep. I snapped a picture of them as they left the hill. They had to continue doing their job, too.

It was now the third week in August, and we got word that we were going to get pulled out in a few days. It didn't make sense to me because there were obviously lots of NVA in the area. Too many as I was to learn later. But that feeling didn't last long, and, like everyone else, I was happy to be leaving. That afternoon we had a special visitor on the hill, and he brought some goodies with him.

A Navy Chaplain, a young Catholic Priest, got off the regular supply chopper with a few big boxes. He enlisted our help in procuring some empty 105 ammo boxes to make an altar. We stacked the boxes on the road behind the crest of the hill to protect it from mortars, and of course I took a picture. The young priest set out his Catholic stuff and put on his priest robe.

Now that I think about it, I believe it really was Sunday. All the guys who had been swearing in Italian accents for almost forty days were now as pure as choirboys. And everyone attended. As I sat on the hill above him, snapping his picture, I thought that this priest had guts to come out here. I never saw anyone on the hill higher in rank than a grunt captain. No journalist and no TV cameramen. Not in Thuong Duc. They were smart to stay away.

After the mass and communion, we walked back up the hill and the priest's returning chopper was about to land. He bid us God's speed and farewell and told us to open the boxes. He said it was a little gift from Battalion for leaving us out here so long.

A couple of the guys started opening the big flat boxes and to our delight it was a hundred and fifty pounds of beefsteak and warm beer. It was only minutes before the wood pallets they came on were broken up and a fire started. A metal pallet made of rebar was used as a grill. We slapped steaks on the grill and used C-2 powder from the leftover powder charges on the howitzers to keep the fire going. The powder bags were cotton cloth, and the powder were really pellets of powder. When you threw a handful of pellets on the fire they would whoosh up in flame and singe the steaks. I think I had five of those steaks. There were none left over, just the bones.

We only had one day left before the pullout when a bunch of us took a truck and the jeep down to the river for one last swim. The children were all there, as usual, when we arrived. They must have had some message system put in place as soon as they saw the truck start down the hill. Kind of a town crier sort of thing. I really enjoyed the kids. They were good kids, and we were good Marines.

We knew the difference between the enemy and these kids. We tried to treat them with the respect they deserved. I would look at the pretty little girls and wonder how they could smile so much when all the things around them were drenched in death. The boys were skinny but strong, and they had a work ethic that would put most American kids to shame.

My little buddy Donn found me, and he wanted to clean my boots. I had him and the others boys wash the jeep instead. I watched them as I swam and wondered what would become of them when we left. The other guys had their favorites too, and I wondered about what they were thinking. I took Donn aside and tried to explain that I was leaving soon, but he didn't speak English, and all I could say was didi, the Vietnamese slang word for go.

I had one of the guys take a picture of Donn and me sitting on the back of the jeep, so I would never forget him. I think he finally understood, because as I said goodbye, I gave him a hug for the first time, and he had a tear in his eye as I left in the jeep.

Donn would be about fifty-three-years old now if he survived the war. I wonder if he ever thinks of me and if he can remember what I look like. I think of him often. The war protesters were wrong when they lumped all Vietnam Vets as baby killers. My guys weren't.

The Sea Knights and Jolly Green Giants started arriving early on 20 August 1968. We had a lot of equipment and ammo to get off the hill, and it would be no easy job. I did not want to spend another night at Thuong Duc because the NVA were probing our wire all night. Rumor had it that we were outnumbered fifty to one and with no other battery in striking distance to protect us, the brass in their wisdom decided to take us out before we were overrun. Watching the huge helicopters lift the trucks and jeep and then the guns and carry them away gave me an unsettling feeling and I thought, "Now would be a good time for an attack, late in the afternoon with no back up."

My fears were finally washed away by the sight of six empty Sea Knights heading back for those of us remaining. The South Vietnamese Rangers and Green Berets would stay one more night and wait for the last 7th Marine platoon to come on the hill the next morning. Then they would all leave together.

I sat on the chopper waiting for it to take off. Forty-eight days in the field. How did we do it? I took a deep sigh and held on as the Sea Knight took off.

21 AUGUST 1968

We were on the last chopper out and it was based on Hill 55, not Hill 10 where Golf battery was located. Waiting until morning to get back to Hill 10 was no big deal because Hill 55 was like being back in the States. Well, at least compared to where we just left. We were extremely happy to be back on Hill 55, John and me and the other three whose names I don't remember. We stowed our gear in the transit hooch and went to the mess hall. It was the first time in forty-eight days that we had eaten real food that wasn't C-rations. Mostly we ate dessert; lots of ice cream and milk. Afterwards we went to the enlisted men's club, a small wood framed tent with a couple of tables, some chairs and a lot of warm beer.

I usually was not much for beer, but this was a special occasion. I had survived another month with the BEAST and besides it didn't take much to get me drunk. I was the only one legally of age to be drinking anyway. We closed the place down and staggered, jokingly, back to the transit hooch around midnight. It was a warm clear night with not much going on in the sky. No "Puff the Magic Dragon" tonight.

I guess we were quite noisy because the others in the hooch told us to shut up, and after a few friendly exchanges of eloquent verbiage, we settled down to sleep. There were no extra cots for us, but no problem. We hadn't slept on a bed for weeks. Curling up on the hard wood floor, I put my poncho liner over my body and as my buddies became quiet, I lay thinking how glad I was leaving Thoung Duc for the last time. It felt good to be alive and back in the world. I thought of home and felt renewed. The last few weeks had taken a strain on me, and I was looking forward to R&R in ten days. I was also looking forward to making sergeant on September 1st. I fell asleep the happiest I'd been since coming to Vietnam.

*

A not so gentle boot in the ribs jarred me awake. My head was spinning from a slight hangover, and for a second I didn't remember where I was. A voice kept asking a question, but I couldn't clear my head. It seemed like I had just fallen asleep, but I soon learned it had been almost six hours. The darkness soon cleared and I was aware of a Marine standing over me in the dim light.

"Are you Corporal Cowart?" he asked.

"Yeah," I answered. "What's going on?"

"Lieutenant wants to see you. Now!"

For the life of me I couldn't figure out what the rush was at 5:45 a.m. I got myself together, grabbed my M-16 and made the walk to the FDC bunker in the dark. I didn't recognize the lieutenant on duty, and he gave me the once over as I entered. I realized how bad I must look to him; long hair, unshaven, dirty red-dirt wrinkled utilities, and jungle hat. He was new and immaculate from head to foot. I thought maybe we had done something wrong last night when we were drunk.

"Corporal Cowart?" He turned away from me as he asked the question as though my dirty combat uniform might be contagious.

"Yes."

He glanced back at me for a second. "Seems as though you Golf Battery guys left a few rounds out at Thoung Duc."

"We didn't leave them. We're FDC," I said

"No matter. A grunt platoon from 7th Marines pulled in there early this morning and found them. Their captain called it in this morning. Your captain back on Hill 10 says you and your FDC team have to go back out there and retrieve them."

"That's bull shit." I said, thoroughly pissed. "How are we supposed to get out there?"

"They're sending choppers to pull the platoon out now. Get your team to the LZ and be on the first one going back out."

"Can't the grunts bring 'em back?"

"Your battery is being punished, corporal! Now get going!"

I turned and walked out. I didn't figure he needed an "aye, aye, sir," and he must have figured I was too salty to bother with. Or maybe he gave me some slack, knowing I was getting screwed by some gun jockey's mistake, and let me go without any further display of officer protocol.

It was getting light as I reappeared from the bunker, and I was pissed. I definitely didn't want to go back out there. Thoung Duc was surrounded by 5000 NVA, and I was scared again. I had thought I was finished with that place. I was even more pissed when I got back to the hooch and woke up the guys. They in turn were pissed as they realized what I was saying. I hurried them along knowing that most of them drank more than me and that they were hung over.

In my haste, I didn't give a thought to my helmet or flak jacket. It was daylight and almost never did the NVA stir in daylight. We left the hooch and made our way down to the LZ. One lone CH-46 was warming up, the one we came in on yesterday afternoon. I didn't say anything to the gunner at the rear; I just went up the ramp and sat down. They evidently were waiting for us, as we lifted off before the ramp started to close.

It was a beautiful morning like most in Vietnam. Only problem was, I couldn't get my head right about what we were doing. I was still pissed that someone had left those rounds. It was a major taboo to leave artillery rounds lying around. The VC could make a booby trap out of them and kill unsuspecting Marines. I kept trying to tell myself that it was no big deal. We'd grab the rounds, get back on the next chopper and come back for a big breakfast at the mess hall.

As we flew west, my pissed mood subsided and was being replaced with an uneasy feeling. I was becoming afraid again. I hated that feeling. For all the times I boarded a chopper and left the world, you'd think I would get used to it. But there it was, that churning deep in the gut. You pretended you weren't afraid, but you knew you were. Afraid. Afraid of the unknown this morning, not necessarily death, but afraid. I hated that feeling. I wanted to be as brave as the rear echelon guys thought I was when they gave me those awe-inspired looks. Those looks that said, " There's Golf Forward, and he just came in from operation. Thank God we don't do what he does, and thanks for this nice safe job in the bunker back in the world."

Shit, if they only knew how scared I was. Still it was better than being a grunt.

I soon saw the Thoung Duc River below. As the chopper blades beat their methodic thump, thump, thump, I looked west as best I could, past the 50-caliber machine gun, and saw the Special Forces camp ahead. All was quiet. Soon I could see the men of the infantry platoon waiting in the ditches and small bunkers that lay around the east border of the landing zone. All of a sudden I felt calm. It was like a homecoming almost. I felt good. I guess the old place wasn't so bad after all. I did have some good times here. The chopper started its final decent, and we readied ourselves for off-loading.

It was noticeably hotter when we ran off the ramp. A squad of grunts were running in as we left. The first Marines I came to directed me over to a captain with binoculars standing next to a jeep with a recoilless rifle on the back. At first I wondered where the jeep came from and then I remembered the South Vietnamese Rangers and Green Berets had one, and that they were still on the hill awaiting removal. But why was it here? My answer came quickly.

A mortar round exploded a couple of hundred yards up the ridge to the west. My sinking feeling came back. What the hell are they shelling us in daylight for? Don't they remember we have jets and choppers? The captain was looking for the spot across the river where the mortar originated. I walked up and introduced myself making sure the captain knew we were FDC and not the gunners who left the rounds.

"I would rather have had the Marines responsible," he said. "I'll have a man show you where they are." Almost before he finished speaking, another round hit 200 yards south of the first round.

"They're adjusting on the landing zone," I said, "In broad daylight."

The captain swept the ridge across the river with the binoculars.

"Yeah," he returned. "Let's get this artillery piece over to the other side of the horseshoe. Corporal, you come with us. I'll show you where the rounds are, and maybe you can show me where the mortars were fired from when you were here before."

"There's no one special place, captain," I replied. "They come from all over."

The Green Beret sergeant who I had seen before, but didn't know his name, drove the jeep to the south side of the hill. As I walked along, the captain asked about the area south across the Song Vu Gia River. His platoon had only been north of the river.

He wasn't much older than me but seemed much older. From the way he spoke to me, I could tell that he respected my opinion in the present predicament.

"I can't tell you much, sir," I said. "I've been on this hill over forty-five days, and we've never been over there. It's the bad lands."

"Well, let's see if we can return a little fire."

The captain searched the southern bank of the river for another minute before giving up. He turned and pointed out where the 105 artillery rounds were.

My guys found the rounds in the back of one of the empty gun positions. They were beehive rounds, point blank rounds that were used at 0 degrees elevation to ward off frontal attacks. They were full of little darts that would rip flesh to shreds. There were five of them, one for each of us.

John and the guys grabbed their rounds and hoisted them on their shoulders. As they made their way back to the LZ, I stayed with the Captain. I pointed out some areas where our battery had seen mortar positions before, and then I waited. After ten minutes we saw the incoming flight of three more Sea Knight CH-46s, but no more mortars. Maybe the NVA thought better of starting trouble. I picked up my artillery round and headed back to the LZ.

My guys were in the tall grass on the south side of the landing zone. I joined them, and the captain returned to the north side. We would go on the chopper first, then as many grunts as possible would follow. We were nervous. I was nervous.

As I knelt in the grass with the artillery round on my shoulder, I could see the choppers ever closer. I could hear them now. My eyes turned to the Marine grunts across the zone. They were forming up to get ready to leave. Some were standing, some were sitting on sand bags, and all were smiling, laughing, joking. No one was concerned about the shelling.

But I was concerned. I looked down at the grass. Fear gripped me once again. I sat there looking at a group of 7th Marines across the landing zone and thinking back on all the events in my life that put me in this little patch of grass in this obscure little country at this particular time. The chopper noise got real loud; I looked back up. It was coming in for a landing.

For some reason I looked toward the grunts again. There was a large puff of red dirt. I strained my eyes thinking it was dust from the Sea Knight. The dirt cloud cleared. The laughing, smiling men were no more. Just bodies on the ground. I felt sick. I felt scared. I felt death.

Then all hell broke loose. The first chopper was landing and the mortars were exploding all around. My buddies and I, being in the open, set off at a run. We were running toward the Sea Knight now, and as the back ramp came down, the machine gunner pushed us toward the wounded. Of course the wounded! They needed to go first. How stupid of us. I dropped that silly beehive round and ran with the others toward the grunts. I could see the pools of blood on the red dirt next to the wounded and dying men as I ran toward the ditch.

There were men going every which way, and I jumped into the ditch with some 7th Marines to get cover and get my bearings. The ditch was about three feet deep. The same time my boots hit the hard red soil, I felt like someone hit me in the back with a baseball bat. I stumbled; my rifle went flying, and then the burn. My back burned. I knew immediately that I had been hit with shrapnel. My first thought was to see if it went through me. I ripped open my shirt and was relieved to see nothing but tanned dirty skin on my chest. I would have passed out right there if I had seen blood. Or at least that is what I remembered thinking weeks later.

Then I suppose I went into shock. I ran up the ditch yelling that I had been hit; there was confusion all around. Explosions, dust clouds and loud sounds. A chopper taking off. Men running for cover. Two Marines I didn't know pulled me down in the ditch and looked at my back. The one who faced me told me what everyone always said, "Not to worry. It's not that bad."

I remember his face. He had a round cherub face. His helmet was on and his cheeks were rosy. I had lost my cover. He was scared, but still his cherub face calmed me.

"There's another chopper comin' in. Can you run?" he asked.

"I think so. I'm okay now," I said. I had my wits about me again.

"Good, 'cause we're not goin' with you," he yelled above the noise. "When the chopper gets here, we're gonna pick you up and get you going. Then you're on your own."

I nodded in the affirmative. I didn't blame him. I wouldn't want to leave the safety of the ditch either if I didn't have to. Within seconds he grabbed me.

"Okay," he shouted. "Here it comes."

I was looking at his face as he and his buddy lifted me to my feet. I still remember that face. I'll never forget it. He calmed me.

They pushed me up and out of the ditch, and I started running. All I could see was dust blowing, but the sound of the chopper was right next to me and I could feel the blade wash. I couldn't see anything. Everything smelled of gunpowder. I remember the torn part of my shirt blowing in the wind as I turned my head momentarily and saw the blood stained tatters gently blowing above my back as I ran. All of a sudden the Sea Knight was ten feet away and five feet up with the ramp coming down. I never broke stride and as the ramp touched ground, my right foot hit the ramp. I ran as far forward as I could, feeling others coming behind me. A big machine gunner on the left side of the chopper grabbed me and flipped me onto the canvas fold-down seat. As I lay there the CH-46 Sea Knight filled up quickly. I felt not quickly enough. I was watching the holes from shrapnel or small arms fire puncturing through the sides of the thin chopper wall. I was lying on my left side so the blood wouldn't fill my good lung, just like we were taught.

I thought, "Get this thing off the ground!" I was never so scared in my life. Then two Marines carried in a third Marine and laid him on the floor below me. He was alive. I remember his face, too. I will never forget his face either. He was looking straight up into the roof. Something made me look down to his legs. He had none below the knees. I stared at those bloody tattered knees and felt ashamed. I felt guilty.

It would be the first of many guilty moments that returned to me over the next fifteen years. I was feeling guilt because I was not wounded as badly as him; or so it seemed. I had all my arms and legs, fingers and toes. He lost his legs. The chopper was full. The ramp was closing. It seemed like an eternity, but was probably more like twenty seconds.

The Sea Knight engines became louder, and we started lifting off. I remember the thing shaking violently and thinking now the chopper was going to get hit and we would all die. I had seen it before, only from the ground. I knew as others did that the first thirty seconds would be the most dangerous. I prayed hard. I didn't want to die at Thuong Duc.

We gained more altitude and made a sharp turn east. I looked around. It was the first time I looked around the whole chopper. I could not believe how many of us were crammed into it. My gaze ended back at my new friend with no legs. I stared first at his tattered knees, wrapped in the thick 4x4 bandages the corpsman carried, then at his face. He never cried. I realized I never cried. I realized, too, that I was no longer in pain. Stiff, uncomfortable, but not severe pain. Years later, in Dental School, I would learn about shock and chemical release by the body.

The helicopter was climbing higher now, and the machine gun started blasting away above my head. Some of the spent casings hit me, but I didn't care. I knew we were high enough to be safe. I looked at my new friend's face again and became calmer.

There was some talking, but not much. No one cried. No one screamed. We were all quiet. I guess they all thought as I did that we were either going to live or die by the wounds we had at that moment, for we had left the battle and were no longer in danger of getting hurt further. There was no use crying because no one could help us until we made DaNang.

I watched my friend's legs and then his face, the whole twenty minutes to DaNang. Alternating between the two bloody areas, I wanted say something to him, but what? What could you say to a young man that had just lost his legs? I felt so sorry for him. One moment I felt glad it wasn't me. The next moment I felt guilty that it wasn't me, and so on throughout the flight.

My new friend's eyes closed as we neared the end of the flight. I feared he might be dead. I looked at his chest, and it moved in a steady rhythm. I felt good for a moment; he was still alive. With tears in my eyes, I prayed for him. The chopper was coming in for a landing at the DaNang Air Base Naval Emergency Unit. I had long since determined that all of the others were wounded more severely then me; guilt may have had a role in that, but since I was the first one on, I was determined to be the last one off. My breathing was becoming labored but steady, and I felt if I was able to run on, I should be able to at least walk off.

We bounced to a landing. It seemed like the Sea Knight emptied in ten seconds. Before I knew it I was the only one left inside.

The machine gunner helped me up and asked if I could walk by myself. I said, “I think I can,” and he helped me out into the sunlight.

The heat from the tarmac hit me hard. The flight had been cool high up. Now the heat was stifling. The helicopter behind me started to lift off and the blade wash almost knocked me down. I ducked instinctively. I felt extremely weak. As I turned I saw the last of the wounded Marines being carried through two blue-green double doors some fifty yards away. I took a few steps then noticed something strange.

On both sides of the double doors, extending quite a distance were two lines of men. Both lines had men dressed in blue shirts and darker blue jeans with white caps on their heads. Obviously Naval personnel. There must have been a hundred in each line or so I remember, and all their eyes were on me. They looked like zombies. They probably were lined up for morning sick call and were witnessing more then they bargained for. That is, if I wasn’t imagining it.

The sailors were left in shock at the carnage they had just seen. I know that now, although at the time I was not happy with them. I could move no further. My breathing was worse, and I knew I needed help. Yet all they could do is stare at me.

"I need some help." I tried to yell it out, but my voice failed me. I fell to my knees, and I think I swore at them as best I could. Still no one moved. They just stared.

All of a sudden the blue doors burst open and the biggest, blackest Marine I had ever seen appeared. He was on crutches and one foot was in a cast or wrap of some kind. He said nothing, but crutched out to me, discarding one crutch. He took me by the hand with his one hand and hoisted me to his shoulder. I could feel the eyes of the sailors on my bloody back. Then he crutched us both back inside and set me down in a chair by the door.

"I'll find you some help," he said. I nodded.

As I slumped in the chair, breathing hard, I look around the huge room. There must have been twenty stretchers between sawhorses with medical personnel manning each, and others running to and fro. There was shouting and general confusion all around. The whole room was green.

I was having real trouble breathing now, but I couldn't see my big black friend anywhere. Finally, I surmised that my lungs must be filling with blood and maybe I was wounded worse than I had thought.

I tried to speak at passers by, but to no avail. I couldn't make sounds, and I couldn't breathe anymore. I grabbed on to the shirttail of the next man walking by and gasped at him. Luckily he realized my dilemma and called for help. Three Navy corpsman rushed over and carried me to one of the vacant stretchers between sawhorses.

"We have a thoracic wound here," one yelled.

A doctor dashed over and looked me over quickly and shouted some orders, sending the corpsman running. Within seconds one was cutting my shirt off and the others returned with surgical instruments and other medical stuff. They work busily, yelling at each other in cross tones. Obviously it was stressful and no fun for them either. I just lay there taking it all in. I was gasping. I needed something positively definitive to happen, and I needed it now.

The doctor and an older man returned. I watched the doctor pick up an instrument and move toward my left chest. I screamed. I scared them, the doctor and the old man.

"Son of a bitch," the doctor screamed at no one in particular. "Didn't you get him numb?"

He had cut me in the chest with his scalpel. The head corpsman, I assume he was because he answered, said that they hadn't had time. The doctor was displeased to say the least. So was I.

"Damn it!" The doctor turned to the old man. "Sorry, Father."

He turned back to me. I was dying.

"We haven't got time," he said, " Grab his arms."

The corpsman and the old chaplain priest held me down and the doctor cut a hole between my fourth and fifth ribs all the way to the lung. God it hurt, worse than the wounding. I think I screamed, but I'm not sure sound came out; I know I squeezed the chaplain's hand real hard. I was scared. I had tears for the first time. It hurt real bad. I will never forget that feeling; that cold sharp scalpel violating me.

"Marine! Look at me!" The doctor was dead serious, his eyes fixed on mine. "Take a deep breath."

What I didn't know is that the doc had slipped a rubber tube into the lung through the hole he had just cut. I took a deep breath and blood squirted upon my chest. I think I started crying.

"Keep taking a breath," he yelled at me, and I did.

I breathed in and the blood squirted out of the tube, but the breath wouldn't stop. I couldn't fill up my lung. The breath went on for what seemed like twenty seconds. When the blood flow ceased, the doctor clamped a forceps onto the tube cutting off the opening.

"Now, breathe in and out like normal," the doctor said. "Does it feel better?"

I had tears in my eyes as I looked at him. It was better. I could breathe again. He handed me another forceps and told me if that one got knocked off to clamp this one on and call for help. I could talk again and said I would. I felt ashamed that I was crying. He turned away, giving some last orders, and then he was gone. I never saw him again.

The old Navy Chaplain told me I was going to be fine now and dried my face. He left, too. They all went off to help the next Marine in need, and wounded Marines were coming in the door again. I was by myself for some minutes. I didn't cry any more, but reflected on what had just happened to me over the last half hour, trying to make sense of it all. I lay there looking up at the green ceiling. I couldn't believe it. I thought I was going to be fine, but I still wasn't sure.

Soon the room filled with more nurses and doctors and corpsmen. They must have sent for re-enforcements. There were more wounded coming in, and as I found out much later, our shelling started a major battle that lasted weeks. It was a continuation of the Tet Offensive that had been going on all of 1968.

Two corpsmen finally came to get me, and each one took an end of the stretcher and lifted me off the sawhorses. They were stressed like the others, and during our brief trip to another part of the hospital, they were continually arguing with one another. I couldn't make out exactly what the problem was, but I remember thinking, "How petty to be arguing about whatever, carrying a guy that had just been all shot up." It was like I wasn't there.

We stopped for some x-rays of my chest and stomach. They lifted me and put the cold x-ray cases under my back and took two shots, and then we were on the move again. I just held my forceps and wondered what was next.

Next was a big room that looked like a huge bathroom. Again it had sawhorses for the stretchers, but with rows of sinks along the wall. There were green garden hoses attached to the sink faucets. They placed my stretcher between two sawhorses and started cutting my trousers and taking off my boots and socks. I loved my boots. I got them brand new the fifth day in Vietnam and after six months they were extremely "salty". They were part of my image, my combat aura. I asked the corpsman to save my boots for me. I didn't care about the clothes, but I wanted the boots. Being "salty" is what all Marines yearn for.

They looked at me like I was crazy, but they finally said they would save them. I knew they were lying, and sure enough, I never did get my boots back. After my clothes were cut away, they took the garden hose and started washing me down. That felt strange and undignified. I could see the dirt and blood pool on the canvas stretcher. When they finished washing and rinsing, they started shaving me down by my private parts. This concerned me and I asked the reason for this.

"You need an operation," they said, "to get out some shrapnel."

This seemed reasonable, but it made me think that I must be wounded worse than I thought. I was wet from head to toe, and the stretcher was wet, too. All I was wearing were my dog tags and the chest tube. I was lying there getting scared again when one of the corpsmen called for another stretcher, and two more young men showed up with it. This time it was a gurney with wheels. The four of them dried me, and then lifted me to the dry gurney. It hurt. I grimaced and kept an eye on my clamped tube as they were moving me. One of the new corpsmen rolled me out of the big bathroom and down the hallway.

It was a busy hallway. He went through double doors and stopped by some curtains. Another person put a tube in my arm and hung a clear bag of liquid above my head on a chrome post. They wheeled me into another room past double doors again.

I remember a huge round light fixture in the ceiling, as I was looking straight up. It was very bright. Quickly I became aware of other people in the room. They were all looking at me when I looked away from the ceiling. They were all wearing blue surgical robes, masks, and head covers. I thought, “Oh, oh, this is it.” An older man, the surgeon, walked over to me and took the forceps out of my hand.

“You won’t need these anymore,” he said. “You’ve got some metal in you that we need to take care of right away.”

He was a calming man, and I felt comfortable in his presence, but there was one thing that I had to ask, something that had been troubling me in between all the prepping for surgery and the arguing corpsman.

“Can I ask you a question before you start?” I said.

“Sure,” he replied.

“When you’re all done, am I staying here? I mean do I have to go back out there again?”

He looked at me and chuckled under his mask. “No,” he answered slowly. “Your war is over. You be a good patient and do what we say, and you will be going back home.”

What a relief. I was ready for anything after that. Bring it on.

He continued. "I'm going to put this mask over your nose and mouth in a moment, and I want you to breathe normally. I'm going to ask you to count backwards from a hundred. Will you do that for me?"

I nodded yes.

"Okay then, here we go." He lifted the mask above my head. I saw the lights in the big fixture above it get brighter, and the mask was lowered toward my face. I never counted backwards. I never remember the mask coming in contact with my face. The last thing I remember is that black mask hovering over me, and then I was out. I guess I was ready to end this chapter in my life. I was so ready, I just passed out. I remember nothing after that. No dreams. No bright guiding lights or out of body experiences. Nothing.

When I awoke there was a Navy nurse next to my bed. It was dark, and I was aware that I was in a large half-moon ward with many other beds. My nurse was strange in that she was wearing a helmet and held a flashlight. I knew she was female because she was talking to me, asking me how I felt. I felt nothing. I was sitting halfway up in bed with a pillow behind my head. I hadn't felt a pillow in two months. I didn't answer her right away because I was focused on all the tubes going in and out of me.

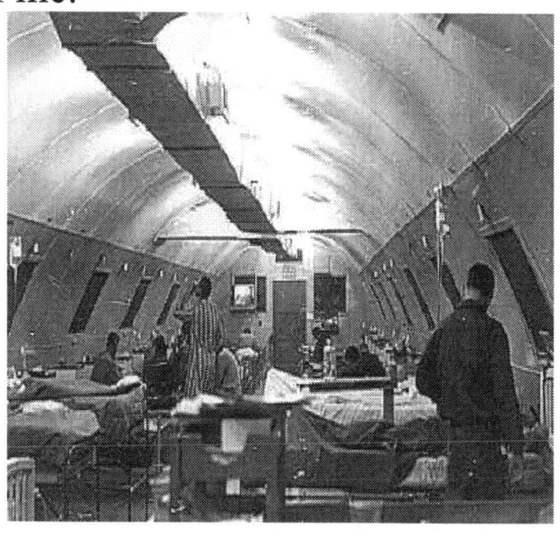

Her flashlight illuminated my body. I had a tube coming out of my nose. The one coming out of my chest was hooked to some sort of suction machine. One tube was coming out of the lower right side of my stomach and one out of my penis. I had tubes in both arms. I had a huge white bandage over the middle of my stomach. This surprised me.

“Why the helmet?” I asked. Just saying those three words exhausted me, and I felt the tube down my throat when I spoke.

“We’ve been getting rocket attacks tonight, but I think they’re over with now. I’m going to give you a shot, and you’re going to sleep some more. Okay?”

I nodded, not wanting to speak again. She wet my arm with alcohol and gave me a shot. Then she smiled and walked away. I looked around fantasizing about what would happen if the NVA broke into our ward. Would they kill us? I was wishing I had my M-16 as I fell asleep.

The morphine kept me asleep for about four hours, I would later learn. When I awoke again the lights were on and the ward had more staff moving from patient to patient. I sat and watched the routine for a while, but it was easiest to look straight ahead. To move my head or any part of my body hurt. There were other Marines in beds across from me and one man I thought was Korean. He didn’t speak English and was having a hard time of it. They were trying to make him understand what they were doing, but he fought them. Two male corpsmen had to hold him while they gave him a shot and put a tube down his nose into his throat. He finally calmed down and the corpsmen started to walk away. As soon as they did the young Korean ripped the tube out of his nose, and started pushing the nurse away.

I was shocked. Now I knew why the surgeon wanted me to be a good patient so I could go home sooner. I told myself I would do everything they wanted and not complain.

The corpsmen returned to the Korean and held him until a doctor came by and put him out with another shot. Soon after, they came to me, asked me how I felt, and had me cough a few times. It hurt, but I did it. Then they had me breathe pure oxygen through a mask for about five minutes. By then I was hurting everywhere on my body, but before I could let them know, they came back with another morphine shot, and I slept again.

Time became confusing, and I was never sure of what time of day it was or how long I stayed in DaNang. At some point I noticed the large bandage covering my stomach. I thought it must be the incision for the surgery they did. On one of my brief periods of being awake, they changed the dressing, and I was shocked to see stainless steel wires instead of sutures. There must have been twenty of them running from my sternum to just above my private areas. Each twisted two or three turns at the top so they would stay in place. The other surprise during this dressing change was the realization that I had wounds on my right side, right hip and right knee.

"Why do I have this bandage on my stomach?" I asked the nurse, even though I knew it was from the surgery.

"They had to take out some metal fragments and repair your liver and kidney," she answered.

"My liver. I thought my lung was the only problem."

"Look here," she said as she helped me move and lift my right side. She pointed to my right side. There were two bandages on my side, two more on my right hip and one on my right knee.

I stared at the wounds.

"You have four nickel and quarter sized holes in your left back. You have these five on your right side. You don't remember getting hit on the right?" she asked.

"No," I answered. "I don't remember that at all." But sure enough, there they were.

"These two little holes on your side did most of the damage inside. That why the doctors went into your tummy."

The only thing I can think of is that something must have hit me on the way to the helicopter, or in the helicopter. I remember the holes popping through the helicopter wall, but not of getting hit by anything. I was in shock, and it may not have registered. I can remember parts of that time vividly, but only parts. The rest is a blur. The talking made me tired, and I was hurting again. She made me stand and walk a few steps, being careful not to dislodge any tubes. I returned to bed, coughed some more, breathed oxygen again, and got my shot.

As I said, time was confusing, but soon I realized I was being moved. They must have kept me heavily drugged because I don't remember much, other than being placed on a gurney and waking up in a more traditional hospital bed with yellow walls. Literally, only seconds of consciousness and then back asleep.

My next awakening found me on a stretcher, and it was noisy and hot. Two men were carrying me up the rear ramp of a huge airplane. A nurse walked at my side caring my plastic bags and tubes above me. All around me I could see stretchers with men in them from floor to ceiling.

They took me halfway in, and put the stretcher with me still in it into some brackets on the side of the airplane bulkhead. There were two stretchers below me and at least two above. The space above me seemed less than a foot from the stretcher above, and my first thought was that I was going to panic in this small space, but fortunately the morphine shot came as soon as they noticed I was awake. I remember nothing more of that flight.

My next memories were so fantastic that at first I thought they were dreams. It wasn't until years later, watching the television show M*A*S*H, that I fully understood what had happened.

I awoke to the loud beating of helicopter blades and saw above me the blur of the blades rotating. I was on a stretcher and had the feeling that I was encased in a plastic dome. I turned on my side and looked down. I was indeed in the air and below me were baseball fields. Yes, baseball fields. The green grass of the outfield surrounding the brown dirt of the infield. The diamond shapes of America's national pastime were everywhere.

I remember having a feeling of dreaming, but in any case I told myself I couldn't deal with all this right now and passed out again. I was flying over Tokyo in a Korean War era helicopter that had the wounded strapped on the outside. Just like the beginning of each M*A*S*H episode in the 1970's.

Soon I awoke in a large hospital ward and was being transferred to a bed in the middle of the room. There were many wounded men here, and I was later to learn that I was in Fort Drake Army hospital in Tokyo, Japan. It was daytime and sunny outside. I had not had windows to look out of for some time, and I was to find out later that day that a week had passed since my wounding. I was happy to learn that I was out of Vietnam, and the nurse told me that when I was well enough, I would be going back to the States.

I was awake for some time that afternoon, as the morphine shot did not come for over an hour. I was sore, but I was enjoying just looking around the ward and being able to look out the window. I also was given ice to chew on and promised that the tube down my nose might come out as soon as the doctor saw me. It didn't happen that afternoon, but the shot put me to sleep.

I awoke during the night and lay there thinking of all that had happened and wondering of my friends. Had they made it? I wondered, too, about the Marine with no legs. There were lots of amputees in the ward, but I could not tell for sure if he was among them. I thought days later that I saw him being wheeled past, outside my window, but I couldn't be sure it was him. I decided that he had made it okay, and told myself it could have been him, so I just believed it was.

As I was thinking all these thoughts, a Marine across the aisle from me started screaming. He was a sergeant, and he was extremely skinny. I had noticed him earlier in the day and read the nametag on his crib. Yes, crib! He was in a crib, like a baby would have, with high sides so he couldn't get out. He was different from the rest of us in that he had no bandages. He had sat curled up all afternoon, shaking at times, and talking to himself at times. Now he was screaming and the duty nurse came over to calm him. He was undoubtedly having a nightmare, and I thought how could a Marine sergeant act this way, but then I realized. There it was. War, in all its glory. I felt so sorry for him after that. I could only wonder what horrors he had lived through. They finally got him calmed down and all was quiet again.

The next day I was moved closer to the corner of the ward. They took the catheter out from my private part, and I started peeing in a bed urinal after that. The Marine next to me was a really nice guy. I don't remember his name, and I'm not sure we ever exchanged names, but he seemed to be the type of guy that could be your best friend. He had lots of issues with his abdomen. He had been gut shot real bad. He couldn't sit up like I was doing now, and he had more tubes going in and out of him than I had. Some tubes were connected to a weird machine that hummed. It wasn't the same machine I had hooked to my chest tube.

He was happy though because his parents were coming to Japan to see him within the next few days. I found it unbelievable that parents could afford a trip to Tokyo, but I was glad for him. I knew my parents could never afford that kind of trip.

The doctor finally came around and after spending a lot of time with my new friend, he came over to me and checked me over. He asked me if I was hungry. I hadn't given that much thought the last week, but I decided that I was. He told me he was going to take one of the two tubes out of my wrist, which he did with minimal discomfort. Then he took the tape off my nose, freeing up the tube into my nose and down my throat.

"Okay," he said, "I'm going to take this tube out, and it will feel a little strange."

I immediately thought this was a lie, but I gathered my courage and was ready. He was right; it *was* strange feeling that tube worm its way back out, but with minimal pain as he pulled it quickly. The good news was that I was now ready to eat again. Dinner that evening were the first bites I had taken in a week. It was just Jell-O and ice cream, but it was a start. I also was getting very cranky with pain as the shots of morphine were coming with less frequency. Finally it was shot time, and it felt like I fell asleep even before the shot was finished.

I awoke later that night to a lot of movement next to me and hushed tones around my new friend's bed. Four or five nurses and doctors were busy working on my friend with makeshift lights. I tipped my head forward to see better, and they had his abdomen wide open. I mean I could see all the guts. There were tubes and clamps going every which way in and out of his guts. They were working frantically, and from their demeanor it was clear that my new friend was in trouble. One of the nurses noticed me watching and quickly pulled a fabric barricade between us so I could no longer see. But I could hear.

They kept up their work for the longest time, and then at one point they all left. The machine wasn't humming any more. They just left the fabric barrier there and left him. I could hear no movement. All was quiet.

Soon it was time for my shot and I fell back asleep. The next morning when I woke up, he was gone. All his personal stuff was gone. I can't tell you how bad that made me feel. His parents were on their way, but he didn't live to see them. That's why they were coming, because he was dying, and they tried to keep him alive long enough to see them. His organs just gave out. I liked him.

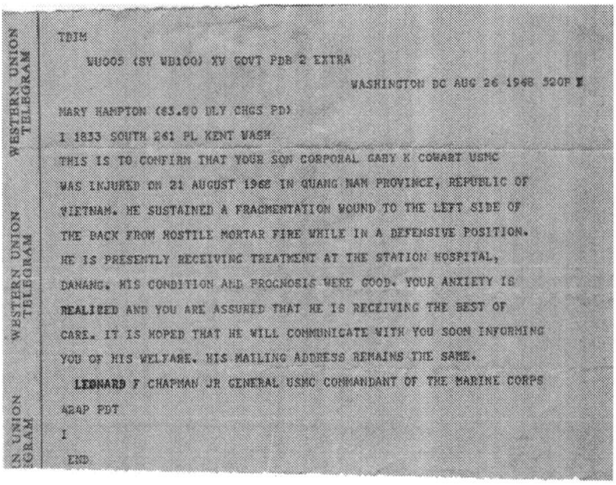

WESTERN UNION TELEGRAM

TDJM

WUOO5 (SY WD100) XV GOVT PDB 2 EXTRA

WASHINGTON DC AUG 26 1968 520P E

MARY HAMPTON (63.80 DLY CHGS PD)

1 1833 SOUTH 261 PL KENT WASH

THIS IS TO CONFIRM THAT YOUR SON CORPORAL GARY K COWART USMC WAS INJURED ON 21 AUGUST 1968 IN QUANG NAM PROVINCE, REPUBLIC OF VIETNAM. HE SUSTAINED A FRAGMENTATION WOUND TO THE LEFT SIDE OF THE BACK FROM HOSTILE MORTAR FIRE WHILE IN A DEFENSIVE POSITION. HE IS PRESENTLY RECEIVING TREATMENT AT THE STATION HOSPITAL, DANANG. HIS CONDITION AND PROGNOSIS WERE GOOD. YOUR ANXIETY IS REALIZED AND YOU ARE ASSURED THAT HE IS RECEIVING THE BEST OF CARE. IT IS HOPED THAT HE WILL COMMUNICATE WITH YOU SOON INFORMING YOU OF HIS WELFARE. HIS MAILING ADDRESS REMAINS THE SAME.

LEONARD F CHAPMAN JR GENERAL USMC COMMANDANT OF THE MARINE CORPS

424P PDT

I

END

It was then that I wondered if my parents knew I had been wounded. Years later I would find the telegram and know from the date that the Navy Department waited five days before they sent the telegram. I assume they wanted to wait and make sure they didn't have to send a second one.

Life in the ward became routine the next week with wounded Marines coming and going daily. There was no time to make friends, and after my experience a couple of nights before, I was okay with that. I looked forward to breakfast, lunch, and dinner, and my pain shots which were down to two a day.

The doctor took the tube out of my chest and stitched it up, only this time with Novocain. I started walking more and was feeling better. Then the shots stopped. I felt strange. Not really painful, but strange. I looked forward to the shot and became irritable when they didn't come around any more. They gave me pills, probably aspirin, and it didn't seem to help. Finally I reached my limit, and I lost my temper with a nurse one morning.

After a heated exchange about pain, I shouted at her, "Just give me the damn shot." She said I couldn't have any more shots. I was pissed. She reminded me in no uncertain terms that she was an Army officer and that I had better not talk that way again. The next time the doc showed up he was even more deliberate then she had been. I didn't know what withdrawal was. I didn't understand drugs at the time, but I learned never to take them again. The withdrawal wasn't worth the temporary good feeling.

I had another setback in my second week as the chest x-ray showed fluid in my lung, and they informed me that I would need the chest tube again only a little higher up. This brought back memories of the first time, and I was feeling depressed.

"Am I going back in the operating room?" I asked.

"No," the doc said. "We can do it here right now."

This really scared me, and I could feel my eyes welling up. I didn't want to cry again, but the doctor didn't give me time to think about it. He gave me some xylocaine and started right in. He was rougher then the first guy was, and he didn't wait for the xylocaine to work all the way. He seemed rushed. He stuck in the tube and sucked out the fluid clamping the tube with a pair of forceps. Big tears rolled out of my eyes, but I didn't make a peep. He saw them, but said nothing. He just moved on to the next guy with a chest problem. The nurse came over and hooked me up to the suction machine again. I think she felt sorry me as she did her work.

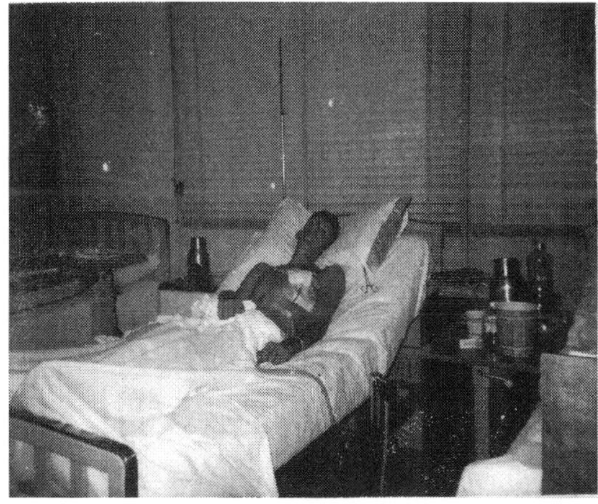

The nurse had a new Polaroid camera and after hooking me up and plugging in the machine, she asked me if I wanted a picture as a keepsake. I said yes, and she snapped a picture of me. It was developed in a minute, and I kept that picture with me wherever I went.

Within a couple of days the chest tube was gone for good. I was now down to one tube; the liver drain tube. This meant I could take longer walks, and they encouraged me to do so. I had my first bowel movement at this time in a bedpan and hated the experience. Peeing was one thing, pooping another. I had the nurse help me to the toilets after that. The walking did me good, and I improved rapidly. I got some stationary and wrote some letters home. They encouraged that too and badgered me until I produced a letter to my mom. Soon I received the word that I would be going back to the States within the next few days.

I woke one morning a few days later and heard that I was leaving after morning rounds. Part of me felt glad, but strangely, part of me didn't want to leave. The ward had been an oasis for me. No heat, no red dirt, no mud, no sleeping in the rain. Compared to Vietnam, the hospital was heaven.

The doctor checked me out and called for a stretcher and two Army guys to put me on the bus. The last few days I had been walking all over the ward, and I asked if I really needed the stretcher. I hated the thought of being pinned between two stretchers with no room to sit up. The doctor watched me walk and said okay.

The bus that was taking us to the airfield had two double seats behind the driver and the rest of the interior was set up for stretchers. Two other Marines and I were allowed to walk out in our pajamas and board the bus.

I sat by myself next to the window, and as we left the Fort Drake compound I got my first good look at Japan. Lots of really small houses and narrow streets. And quite a few baseball fields. My dream-like vision of the helicopter came back to me, and I knew I had really looked down and seen baseball fields although at the time I still was at a loss for how I was able to look out of a helicopter so easily.

The ride to the field took about an hour. When we got to the Air Force base, the bus headed directly to the tarmac. We pulled up close to a C-130 Air Force transport. It must have been the same type of plane I came to Japan on, because they were loading stretchers four or five high on the bulkheads. An Air Force sergeant came aboard the bus and had us three walking wounded sit outside on a bench while they got the stretchers loaded first. We could hear him calling names and guys answering from their stretchers. As each Marine answered, two Airmen would take him into the plane.

More buses came and went and finally our bus was empty. The sergeant came out of the bus and headed toward the three of us who were left.

"Is one of you Corporal Cowart?" he asked.

"Yes." I raised my hand.

"My list says you're suppose to be on a stretcher," he said. "I can't let you go until the flight doctor checks you."

He called the other two names and the two who had been my companions for the last hour or so boarded the plane. It was really hot sitting on the bench with no shade, and I was beginning to wonder if I had been wise to resist the stretcher.

Finally a young doctor came out of the plane with the sergeant and came over to me. He asked me how I was doing, and I told him I was hot and thirsty. He opened my pajama tops and checked the two stitched-up chest tube wounds. He looked at the liver drain and the twenty some odd stainless steel stitches on my stomach and again asked me how I felt. The metal stitches were so bright in the intense sunlight I could barely look at them.

"I feel good, sir," I answered. "I would rather sit in a chair and be able to walk around once in awhile. They told me that it was going to be a fifteen hour flight."

He chuckled and turned to the sergeant. "Let him on board and find him a seat, but have another stretcher posted in case we need to put him down." He turned and walked back to the plane.

"Let's go," the sergeant said.

I got up and walked toward the plane following the sergeant. The noise of the engines and the blast from them blew my hair and I realized that my hair had gotten pretty long for Marine Corps standards. As we started up the ramp a pretty nurse came out with a Dixie cup full of cold water and when she handed it to me, I thanked her. It was good and cold. The doctor must have told her I was thirsty. I looked around for him, but with all the rows of stretchers he was nowhere to be seen.

The sergeant motioned me forward, and we went to the front of the plane. There were four rows of seats facing backwards toward the tail. The plane was huge inside with no windows to speak of. If I remember correctly, there were four rows of stretchers and two aisles where nurses and doctors walked back and forth tending to the men.

There were only a couple of other passengers besides the few walking wounded, and I had no one close to where I sat. I chose the last row next to the stretchers so I could stretch my long skinny legs out. The seat adjusted back a little and was comfortable for the most part. It was noisy, but cool inside out of the sun.

Before long, a nurse came over and gave me a blanket and asked how I was doing. I was fine. The ramp at the rear of the plane started to close, and the long flight home began.

Most of the time I slept. I don't remember eating or going to the bathroom much. It took more like twenty hours to fly home. I do remember getting water and pain-meds, and since my memory of that time is foggy at best, I have to assume I was given some sleep-meds as well. When we landed at Travis Air Force Base, north of San Francisco, it was three o'clock in the morning and pitch black outside. During the landing, I woke up on a stretcher, and the medical staff asked that I stay there for the transfer to buses that would take us to the base hospital.

After the plane came to a stop and the big rear door opened, I realized that most of the wounded men were awake. Air Force men boarded and methodically started removing the stretchers and placing them on buses. When they took me, I laid back and listened to the wounded men around me. Some shouted for joy and some were quiet with tears. Some reached their arms down to touch the ground. All were happy.

No one was there to greet us. No one welcomed us home. We shared that experience like we had combat: Marines, together, taking care of each other.

At the moment, being alive and back in the world was enough. The lack of appreciation for what we had experienced and sacrificed would come much later. Some would never get over it. Many would never re-adjust to the States. All of us left a lot of ourselves, our youth, and our innocence back in Vietnam. War destroys so much.

I would hide my service in this war from all my college friends for four years, and then in Dental School I met two men who were veterans like me. One was a helicopter pilot. All three of us became good friends.

The next day after we landed back in the States, I was transferred to Oakland Naval hospital, where I made many friends in my four-month stay. One was a young candy-striper, a beautiful young high school senior who made me her project. She helped me heal in mind and body.

I will never forget her, or the doctors, the nurses, the corpsman, the men in 3rd Battalion, 11th Marines artillery, or the 7th Marines infantry who fought so bravely along side us. I won't forget the Thuong Duc children, the Continental Flight Attendants who flew us to war, my drill instructors, and all my Marine brothers. I could never forget any of them just like I will never forget Vietnam or the blood from both sides that was shed there and left on the red dirt.

My life began again.

ACRONYM GLOSSARY

AFB – Air Force Base
Amtrak – Amphibious Tracked Vehicle
AWOL – Absent Without Leave
CH-46 – Sea Knight Helicopter
Cpl – Corporal
C-rations – now known as MREs (Meals Ready to Eat)
DI – Drill Instructor
DMZ – Demilitarized Zone
E-Tools – Entrenching Tools
FDC – Fire Direction Control; Fire Direction Center
GySgt – Gunnery Sergeant
HE shells – High Energy Shells
HQ – Headquarters
ID card – Identity card
ITR – Infantry Training Regiment
KIA – Killed In Action
LA – Los Angeles
LAW – Light Antitank Weapon
LP – Listening Post
Lt – Lieutenant
LZ – Landing Zone
M*A*S*H* - Mobile Army Surgical Hospital
MCRD – Marine Corps Recruiting Depot (San Diego)
MFs – Mother F*****s
MP – Military Police
MOS – Military Occupational Specialty
NCO – Non-Commissioned Officer
NFL – National Football League
NVA – North Vietnamese Army
PFC – Private First Class
PRC – Portable Radio Communication
PX – Post Exchange
RPG – Rocket Propelled Grenade
R&R – Rest and Relaxation
Sgt - Sergeant
SP – Self Propelled
SSgt – Staff Sergeant

VC – Viet Cong
WP – White Phosphorus
WWI – World War I
WWII – World War II

Acknowledgements

Pictures by G. K. Cowart

Thanks to those Marines that spurred my memory:

Charlie Cruz

John Hill

Jesus Castillo

Hank Finch

Charles Townsend
John Stenhouse

Norris Keirn

Eric Visser

Greg Williams

Larry Binns

Jack Wells

NAS Da Nang Pictures by

Corpsman Jim Chaffee

A request :

If any one reading this book knows of a Vietnam Veteran Marine by the name of **Charles Cruz**, or **John Hill**, from California, or **Jesus Castillo**, from either Texas, New Mexico, or Arizona and they served with "G" battery 3/11 in 1968, please have them contact me at,

gkcowart@yahoo.com

Thank you,

Gary K. Cowart

Made in the USA
Lexington, KY
22 November 2012